Minecraft®
FOR
DUMMIES®
PORTABLE EDITION

by Jacob Cordeiro

WILEY

John Wiley & Sons, Inc.

Minecraft® For Dummies®, Portable Edition

Published by
John Wiley & Sons, Inc.
111 River Street
Hoboken, NJ 07030-5774
www.wiley.com

Copyright © 2013 by John Wiley & Sons, Inc., Hoboken, New Jersey

Published by John Wiley & Sons, Inc., Hoboken, New Jersey

Published simultaneously in Canada

For general information on our other products and services, please contact our Customer Care Department within the U.S. at 877-762-2974, outside the U.S. at 317-572-3993, or fax 317-572-4002.

For technical support, please visit www.wiley.com/techsupport.

Wiley publishes in a variety of print and electronic formats and by print-on-demand. Some material included with standard print versions of this book may not be included in e-books or in print-on-demand. If this book refers to media such as a CD or DVD that is not included in the version you purchased, you may download this material at http://booksupport.wiley.com. For more information about Wiley products, visit www.wiley.com.

Library of Congress Control Number: 2012955540

ISBN 978-1-118-53714-5 (pbk); ISBN 978-1-118-53713-8 (ebk); ISBN 978-1-118-53715-2 (ebk); ISBN 978-1-118-53716-9 (ebk)

Manufactured in the United States of America

14 13 12

WILEY

About the Author

Jacob Cordeiro has been playing Minecraft since the Alpha pre-release. Jacob attends Stanford Online High School and won an award for his game entry in the 2011 Scholastic Art and Writing competition.

Dedication

To my mom — thank you for all your support throughout the writing of this book. You have raised me to reach toward my own goals and have guided me with truth and respect, and I owe you my awesome life.

To my dad — thank you for giving me all the resources I ever could have wanted and for sparking my interest in both computer games and writing.

To Mrs. Melanie Nelson, who made all of this possible by placing her trust in me and taking the time to get me off the ground — you found me this opportunity, and you taught me how to appreciate computer games in your Game Maker group.

Finally, to all of my friends and, specifically, Alec, Sam, Renee, Noel, and my brother, Adam, who, throughout both school and leisure, have been great peers.

Author's Acknowledgments

Thanks to everyone I worked with — Amy Fandrei, for taking a chance in hiring me; and Kim Darosett and Rebecca Whitney, who were very considerate in making the process easier for me and whose efforts made *Minecraft For Dummies*, Portable Edition a project to be proud of for a long time. I also want to thank my friend, Alec Hendricks, who was helping me write a book before I even knew it.

My instructors and mentors gave me the skills necessary for writing this book, and Mrs. Nelson, who's known me my whole life, put her word in to give me this opportunity.

Also, thanks to my parents and brother, who went as far as to change their own schedules to fit mine. You respected me enough to make my own choices with my time, and both high school and this book have been so much easier because of that choice.

Publisher's Acknowledgments

We're proud of this book; please send us your comments at http://dummies.custhelp.com. For other comments, please contact our Customer Care Department within the U.S. at 877-762-2974, outside the U.S. at 317-572-3993, or fax 317-572-4002.

Some of the people who helped bring this book to market include the following:

Acquisitions and Editorial

Senior Project Editor: Kim Darosett

Acquisitions Editor: Amy Fandrei

Copy Editor: Rebecca Whitney

Technical Editor: Alec Hendricks

Senior Editorial Manager: Leah Michael

Editorial Assistant: Annie Sullivan

Sr. Editorial Assistant: Cherie Case

Cover Photo: Image courtesy of Jacob Cordeiro

Composition Services

Senior Project Coordinator: Kristie Rees

Layout and Graphics: Jennifer Creasey

Proofreaders: Cynthia Fields, John Greenough

Indexer: Potomac Indexing, LLC

Publishing and Editorial for Technology Dummies

Richard Swadley, Vice President and Executive Group Publisher

Andy Cummings, Vice President and Publisher

Mary Bednarek, Executive Acquisitions Director

Mary C. Corder, Editorial Director

Publishing for Consumer Dummies

Kathleen Nebenhaus, Vice President and Executive Publisher

Composition Services

Debbie Stailey, Director of Composition Services

Contents at a Glance

Table of Contents

Introduction

*I*f you enjoy games about building, survival, engineering, and adventuring, Minecraft is for you. Having attracted more than 9 million players, Minecraft is a loose-ended yet adventurous sandbox game that becomes whatever you make of it.

Minecraft is about gathering resources and building structures while facing monsters. The world of Minecraft is composed of cubic blocks, which you can break and replace to build houses and craft items. That's all there is to it. The game has evolved to become so balanced and complex that it has attracted millions of satisfied fans. While skimming or scouring *Minecraft For Dummies,* Portable Edition, you can apply every bit of Minecraft information you need to start playing the game to your liking.

About This Book

This book assumes no knowledge of Minecraft, and it can guide you from registering a Minecraft account to crafting various items to building automatic farms and giant buildings and machines, all with an assortment of basic building blocks.

Although Minecraft has a gigantic community of players who design their own third-party programs, *Minecraft For Dummies,* Portable Edition, focuses primarily on the game itself. This book is a helpful resource for new Minecraft players to gain momentum in the game and recall information they may have otherwise forgotten. Though this book goes only so far in giving strategic guidance, leaving most of the game to the player's creativity, you can find extensive notes in this book on many of Minecraft's most complex systems and game components.

Minecraft continually releases new updates and features — this book is accurate to Minecraft version 1.4.5. Because later Minecraft updates aren't likely to change the primary game mechanics, this book encompasses most of Minecraft's main features.

Foolish Assumptions

Rather than try to consider every single type of reader who might pick up this book, I've made certain assumptions about you, the reader:

- You have a computer, and you know how to use it.
- You know what a web browser is, and you can surf the web.
- You have an e-mail address, and you know how to use it.
- Your computer can download and run Java programs.
- You have a functioning keyboard and computer mouse.

Icons Used in This Book

I've placed various icons in the margins of this book to point out specific information that you may find useful:

This icon calls attention to any tip or trick that you can use to enhance the gameplay.

This icon emphasizes points that you should attempt to retain in your memory. If you can remember these special points, you'll be a better player.

If you see this icon, read its information! Warnings can prevent you from making a big mistake that can be hazardous to your Minecraft world (or your computer).

You can safely skip this geeky stuff. However, it deserved a place in the book, so you may be interested in reading it.

Conventions Used in This Book

In *Minecraft For Dummies,* I use numbered steps, bullet lists, and screen shots for your reference. I also provide a few sidebars containing information that's non-essential but may help you understand a topic a little better. Web addresses appear in a special monotype font that looks like this:

```
www.dummies.com
```

Bonus Content at Dummies.com

You can find a free bonus chapter, "Exploring Other Blocks and Items," and the appendix, "Blocks, Items, and Crafting Recipes," available for download at

```
www.dummies.com/go/minecraftfd
```

Where to Go from Here

Reading *Minecraft For Dummies,* Portable Edition, from cover to cover provides a lot of useful information, but you can just as easily skip around to find specific topics of interest to you. If you're new to Minecraft and you want to know what the game is all about, read Chapters 1 through 3 and skim most of the other ones. They delve into more detail than is necessary at first. You can always return to those bits later.

If you're more experienced in Minecraft and you want to deepen your understanding (if you haven't done so already), simply skim the first three chapters and find some interesting topics later in the book. Also, be sure to check out Chapter 11, of course, which has a top ten list of Minecraft tips.

Occasionally, Wiley's technology books are updated. If this book has technical updates, they'll be posted at

```
www.dummies.com/go/minecraftfdupdates
```

1

Entering Minecraft

In This Chapter

▶ Registering your account
▶ Buying and downloading Minecraft
▶ Starting your first game
▶ Recognizing the basic controls

*I*n the sandbox-survival game of Minecraft, you build structures, fight monsters, collect items, mine minerals, and work toward your own goals. This 3-D, grid-based game features naturally generated landscapes and challenges.

In *Survival mode,* you must manage your resources and acquire increasingly useful items to advance through the game. In *Creative mode,* you can build or design whatever structure, setup, or invention you want in your personal universe. However, most of the information you need is found in Survival mode. This chapter explains how to obtain Minecraft, start on a Survival world, and familiarize yourself with the basic game controls.

Registering a Minecraft Account

To jump into the action, you first have to register a Minecraft account. Then you can play in Demo mode or upgrade to a Premium account, which you need for the full version. Follow these steps to register an account:

> **1. Go to** `http://minecraft.net.`
>
> The Minecraft home page opens.

2. **Click the Register link in the upper-right corner of the page.**

   The Register New Mojang Account page appears.

3. **Fill out all the information requested in the text boxes, specify your date of birth, and answer the security questions.**

4. **Click the Register button to finish.**

5. **Check the e-mail account you entered for a verification message from Minecraft.**

6. **Click the link provided in the e-mail to complete your registration.**

   Check out the next section to find out how to purchase the game.

Purchasing and Installing Minecraft

To buy and install the game, log in to your account at http://minecraft.net. (See the preceding section for details on registering.) Then follow these steps:

1. **Click the large Buy Now button on the home page.**

   The Minecraft Store page opens.

2. **Click the Buy Minecraft for This Account option in the upper-left corner of the store, as shown in Figure 1-1.**

   At the time of this writing, the cost of the game is $26.95.

   If you can't click the button, you may not be logged in (or you may have already bought the game).

3. **Fill out your payment information and then click the Proceed to Checkout button.**

Figure 1-1: Buying the game

4. **Follow the necessary steps to complete your purchase.**

5. **Return to the Minecraft home page. On the right side of the screen, the large Buy Now button should now be labeled Download Now. Click this button to open the Download page.**

6. **If you're using Windows, click the download and save the file anywhere on your computer.**

   To view instructions for other operating systems, click the Show All Platforms button.

7. **Double-click the file to install the game.**

Your payment is immediately attributed to your account, so, if necessary, you can download the file again for free. The Minecraft home page also gives you the option to play from your browser — click the link under the Download Now button.

Playing the Game

After you install Minecraft, you're ready to start playing the game. To start, run the launcher you downloaded.

Logging in and operating the main menu

The launcher opens the news screen, which displays game updates and links. Enter your username and password in the lower-right corner and click Log In to continue to the main menu, as shown in Figure 1-2.

Figure 1-2: Main menu

This list describes what you can do after you click the buttons on the main menu:

✔ **SinglePlayer:** Start or continue a basic game. This chapter covers the options for starting a game in SinglePlayer mode.

✔ **MultiPlayer:** Join other players online. You can find more information about MultiPlayer mode in Chapter 9.

✔ **Languages:** Change the language of the text in Minecraft. This tiny button next to Options holds a speech bubble containing a globe.

✔ **Options:** Manage game options such as sound, graphics, mouse controls, difficulty levels, and general settings.

✔ **Quit Game:** Close the window, unless you're in In-Browser mode.

Starting your first game in SinglePlayer mode

To start your first game in SinglePlayer mode, follow these steps:

1. **Click the Singleplayer button to view a list of all your worlds.**

   If you're just starting out in Minecraft, this list should be empty.

2. **Click the Create New World button to start a new game.**

   The world-creation page appears, as shown in Figure 1-3.

Figure 1-3: Creating a new world

3. **In the World Name text box, type whatever name you want and click the Create New World button at the bottom.**

   The Game Mode and More World Options buttons are covered in Chapter 10.

To turn on game *cheats,* special powers that provide a more casual experience, click the More World Options button, and then click the Allow Cheats button to turn cheats on or off. Cheats make the game stress-free when you're getting started by giving you more control over the world. Chapter 2 explains how to use a basic cheat for surviving your first game.

When you finish creating your world, the game automatically starts by generating the world and placing your *avatar* (character) in it.

Understanding basic controls

The world of Minecraft, shown in Figure 1-4, is made of cubic *blocks,* materials such as dirt or stone that you can break down and rebuild into houses or craft into useful items. A block made of a material such as sand is referred to as a *sand block.* Because the side length of every block measures 1 meter, most distances are measured in blocks as well: If you read about an object that's located "three blocks up," it's the distance from the ground to the top of a stack of three blocks.

In addition to building and crafting, you have to defend against monsters and eventually face them head-on. As the game progresses, your goal becomes less about surviving and more about building structures, gathering resources, and facing challenges to gain access to more blocks and items.

Figure 1-4: The look and feel of Minecraft

To survive, you have to know how to move around, attack enemies, and manipulate the blocks that comprise the world. Table 1-1 lists the default key assignments for each control.

If you reassign any major keys, you may cause confusion later in the game.

Table 1-1   Default Controls in Minecraft

Action	Control	What Happens When You Use It
Pause	Esc	The game pauses (only in SinglePlayer mode), and the Game menu opens. Click Options⇨Controls to change the controls for certain actions. You can also close menus and other in-game screens.
Forward	W	Your avatar moves forward when this key is held down. Double-tapping the W key makes the character sprint — and makes the avatar hungry, as explained in Chapter 3.
Back	S	Your avatar backs up.
Left	A	Your avatar moves to the left.
Right	D	Your avatar moves to the right.
Look	Mouse move-ment	Your avatar looks around. The Forward control always makes the avatar move in the direction you're looking.
Jump	Space	Your avatar jumps over one block at a time. Use this control while moving to make your way around rough terrain or jump over gaps. Jump while sprinting to leap over a great distance! Hold down this button while swimming to swim upward or keep your avatar's head above water.
Attack	Left mouse button	Your character attacks in the direction of the crosshair in the middle of the screen. Tap the button to punch nearby entities, or hold down the button to break nearby blocks.
Drop	Q	Your character drops the selected item, as explained in Chapter 2.

(continued)

Table 1-1 *(continued)*

Action	Control	What Happens When You Use It
Sneak	Left Shift	Your character moves slower, but cannot walk off edges. In MultiPlayer mode (Chapter 9), other players can't see your avatar's name tag if a block is in the way.
Inventory	E	Your avatar's inventory is shown, described in Chapter 2, and any open menus except the Pause menu are closed.
Chat	T	The Chat menu opens. Type a message, and then press Enter to talk to friends in multiplayer worlds or implement cheat commands.
List Players	L	A list of all players in the world is shown (disabled in single-player worlds).
Pick Block	Middle mouse button	Click nearby blocks or entities with the middle mouse button to put them into the bottom row of your inventory, possibly replacing the selected item. It works only in Creative mode (Chapter 6). If your mouse has no middle button, reassign this key on the Pause menu.
Command	/	The Chat menu opens and shows a slash mark (/), used for cheat commands.
Hide GUI	F1	All visual images are turned off, except for the player's view of the world (used for capturing imagery).
Screenshot	F2	A screen shot of the current view is taken (Chapter 10).
View Performance	Shift+F3	(Rarely used.) You can view the game performance, and everything on the F3 menu.
View Statistics	F3	Your character's coordinates, current biome, and other information are shown. The y-axis points upward.
Change View	F5	The camera view changes between first-person view (recommended), third-person view, and in front of the avatar looking back at the avatar.
Smooth Movement	F8	This makes the mouse cursor move more smoothly (used for recording).

Walk around and explore the world. After you get the hang of using the controls and you're prepared to immerse yourself in the fun and challenge of the real game, it's time to figure out how to survive. Chapter 2 gives you the lowdown on surviving your first night.

Watching the Heads-Up Display (HUD)

The little arrangement at the bottom of the screen, is known as the Heads-Up Display, or HUD. To show the important details of your character, the HUD features these four sections, as shown in Figure 1-5:

Figure 1-5: Heads-Up Display

✔ **Health bar:** These ten hearts monitor the health of your avatar. As your avatar incurs damage, the hearts disappear. After all ten are depleted, your avatar dies and reappears at its *spawn point,* a position that can be changed by sleeping in a bed.

Your avatar can take damage by falling from ledges four blocks tall, colliding with harmful blocks or entities, or succumbing to other dangers such as drowning. When you equip yourself with armor (see Chapter 4), the Armor bar appears over the Health bar, indicating the protective value of your armor.

✔ **Inventory:** These nine squares contain items you've collected, and they're the only squares in the inventory that you can access without pressing E. You can use the 1–9 keys or the scroll wheel to select items, and right-click to use them. If you're using a sword or a tool for breaking blocks faster (such as an axe), the item will automatically function when you left-click. (I discuss the inventory in more detail in Chapter 2.)

✔ **Experience**: The green Experience bar fills up when you collect *experience orbs.* These orbs appear naturally whenever you defeat monsters, smelt items in a furnace, breed animals, or mine any ore except iron or gold. When the bar is full, a number appears or increases over it, indicating your experience level. You can spend levels with anvils (detailed in the bonus chapter, available for download at www.dummies.com/go/minecraftfd) or enchantment tables (detailed in Chapter 6), but you will lose them if you die.

✔ **Hunger bar:** This bar represents your food supply. The emptier the bar, the hungrier you are. Hunger is an important concept to understand, so it's covered in Chapter 3.

✔ **Breath:** When your avatar's head goes underwater, ten bubbles appear just above your Hunger bar and begin to pop one by one. This signifies how long you can hold your breath; if all the bubbles are gone and you're still underwater, your Health bar begins to deplete.

Carefully monitor the Health and Hunger bars, and organize your inventory slots for easy access.

2
Planning for Your First Night

In This Chapter

▷ Concocting a plan of action

▷ Acquiring resources

▷ Building a base of operations

▷ Surviving a day and a night

*A*fter you create a new world in Minecraft, as outlined in Chapter 1, the first order of business is to survive the first night. A Minecraft day lasts for 20 minutes; there are 10-minute daytimes and 3 minutes of sunrise and sunset, during which the player can prepare for the 7-minute nights, when dangerous monsters spawn in the darkness. This chapter helps you survive your first experience; I explain what to expect on your first night — and how to spend your remaining minutes of daylight preparing.

Devising a Game Plan

After your avatar appears, you need to find a living space with some trees and a suitable area for building (usually flat). Always locate trees when starting a game, because you use wooden materials to craft most of the items you need. To survive your first night, craft these elements:

✔ Crafting table (or workbench, used for building)

✔ Storage chest

✔ Shelter with a door

You can also craft useful, but non-essential items for your first night:

- ✔ Wooden and stone tools
- ✔ Torches
- ✔ Furnace
- ✔ Bed

The rest of this chapter explains how to craft these items.

When you start creating your own world, you may discover that the sun is setting too quickly. If that's the case, you can press Esc to open the Pause menu and choose Options⚑ Difficulty repeatedly until it reads `Difficulty: Peaceful`. This option makes the world much safer and causes your health to regenerate. Alternatively, if you enable cheats for your world (read more about cheats in Chapter 1), press T, type **/time set 0**, and press Enter to cause an early sunrise.

Using Your Inventory

Before you start gathering materials and crafting items, you should know how to manage the inventory screen. The nine squares at the bottom of the game screen display items you've obtained. For example, if you break a block like wood or dirt (see Chapter 1 for basic controls), an item pops out that is automatically picked up, causing it to appear in one of your inventory squares. The row of squares at the bottom of the game screen represents a quarter of your inventory.

To see your entire inventory, as shown in Figure 2-1, press E (or the corresponding key binding, as described in Chapter 1).

You should be familiar with these four components of the inventory:

- ✔ **Inventory slots:** The four rows of squares at the bottom of the screen, where you see your items. You select the items in the bottom row outside the inventory screen with the 1–9 keys on the keyboard or the scroll wheel.

✏ **Crafting grid:** A 2-by-2 square, followed by an arrow pointing toward another square to the right. When you want to craft basic items, such as torches or mushroom stew, place the ingredients on the grid to make the result appear on the other side of the arrow.

✏ **Character portrait:** A small screen showing what your character looks like now. This portrait can change when your character sits or sleeps, wears armor, gets hit by arrows, drinks invisibility potions, catches fire, and more.

✏ **Armor slots:** The four squares in the upper-left corner, representing a helmet, a suit, leggings, and boots. When you obtain armor later in the game, you can place it in these slots; shift-clicking a piece of armor will automatically equip it in the corresponding slot. See Chapter 3 for more information about armor.

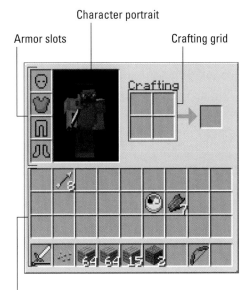

Character portrait

Armor slots

Crafting grid

Inventory slots

Figure 2-1: Inventory screen

Because most items are *stackable,* several similar items such as wooden planks or steak can share the same inventory slot; an item may have a white number next to it in your inventory, indicating how many you have. Most stackable items cannot exceed a *64-stack,* or 64 items in one space. Tools, weapons, and armor do not stack, and some items such as ender pearls or snowballs cannot exceed a 16-stack.

Manipulating Your Inventory

While viewing your full inventory, you can use these basic commands for manipulating items in your inventory:

- ✓ **Pick up the items in an inventory square:** Click a square in the inventory to pick up the items there.

- ✓ **Pick up half of the items in an inventory square**: Right-click a square in the inventory to pick up half (rounded up) of the items there.

- ✓ **Place all items you're holding:** While holding an item or a stack of items, click an empty square to place the item(s) there.

- ✓ **Place a single item that you're holding:** While holding a stack of items, right-click an empty square to place *one* of the items there. The rest remain on the cursor. Right-click several times to place several items.

In addition, while holding an item, you can click outside of the inventory screen to drop the item on the ground. While outside the inventory screen, you can press the 1–9 keys to select an item from the bottom row of your inventory and then press Q to drop it. If you do this with a stack of items, only one item is thrown.

If you're just starting out with Minecraft, break nearby blocks (as described in the section "Harvesting trees," later in this chapter) and move them around in the inventory to get familiar with it.

Setting Up for Your First Night

You should complete a few tasks before nightfall. Start with the essentials, which I discuss in detail in this section:

- **Harvest trees.** Then you can gather wooden planks.
- **Build a crafting table.** It starts off your production.
- **Build a chest.** It keeps your items from being lost.
- **Construct a shelter.** It keeps *you* safe from being attacked.

Harvesting trees

Start the crafting process by chopping down nearby trees. Everything you need to build your shelter requires some form of wood, and the most efficient way to get it is to harvest trees. Look for a place with a good number of trees. (If you're too far away from any plants, you may want to create a new world.)

To start, chop down a couple of trees, which are made of wood blocks and leaf blocks. To break a block from the tree, follow these steps:

1. **Walk up to a tree.**

   See Chapter 1 for a rundown of the basic controls for moving in Minecraft.

2. **Using the mouse, position the crosshair over a block in the tree.**

3. **Click and hold the left mouse button to start punching the block until it breaks.**

4. **Collect the item that appears.**

   The item should come directly to you, but if you're too far away, just walk up to the item to collect it. The resource is added to the inventory at the bottom of the screen.

Ignore the leaves on the tree for now because they decay naturally with nothing supporting them. Destroyed leaf blocks sometimes give sapling items, which you don't need for crafting the essential items covered in this chapter.

Building a crafting table, chest, and shelter

The crafting table and storage chest require wooden planks to build. Follow these steps to use the wood blocks you've gathered (as described in the previous section) to produce wooden planks:

1. **Press E to display the inventory screen.**

2. **Click a square containing wood blocks to pick them up, and then click an empty square in your crafting grid to place them there.**

   Four wooden planks appear next to the grid, as shown in Figure 2-2.

Figure 2-2: Crafting planks

3. **Click the square that contains the planks.**

   One wood block disappears, but four wooden planks appear on the mouse cursor!

4. **Click the square that contains the planks a few more times to pick up all the planks you can, or Shift-click to send all the planks directly to the inventory.**

You can use these planks as building blocks, or use them to build a crafting table and chest.

Crafting table

Your avatar's crafting grid is a 2-by-2 square (refer to Figure 2-2); however, many items you need to survive require a 3-by-3 grid to craft. To unlock this larger grid, you build a crafting table. Follow these steps to build a crafting table, or workbench:

1. **Press E to open the inventory screen.**

2. **Click a square containing your planks, and then right-click each square in the crafting grid to distribute four planks into the squares.**

   A crafting table appears on the right, as shown in Figure 2-3.

Figure 2-3: The crafting table

3. **Click the crafting table to pick it up, and then click a square in the bottom row of the inventory to place the table there.**

   You can access items outside your inventory screen only if they're on the bottom row. This row is always displayed at the bottom of the game screen.

4. **Press E or Esc to close the inventory.**

5. **Use the 1–9 keys or the scroll wheel to select the crafting table.**

   A thick, white outline appears around the crafting table.

You can use either the number keys or the scroll wheel to select items from the bottom row of the inventory. Place the most useful items in the slots you can quickly access.

6. **Right-click a nearby surface to place the crafting table there.**

Right-click the crafting table to view a screen similar to the inventory, with an expanded crafting grid. You use this grid for all the crafting recipes in the game, including the chest, described next.

Chest

You can place the chest, which is a storage unit, in your world and fill it with items. The benefit is that you drop all items when your avatar dies, but *not* the items in your storage chests.

You can craft a chest by following these steps:

1. **Right-click the crafting table to view the expanded crafting grid.**

2. **Confirm that you have at least eight wooden planks.**

   If you don't, chop down more trees, and then right-click the crafting table.

3. **Click your wooden planks to pick them up and right-click every square, except the center one, in the crafting grid.**

   This arrangement is for crafting a chest. The chest appears to the right of the arrow.

4. **Click the chest to pick it up, and then click a square in the bottom row of your inventory to place the chest there.**

5. **Press E or Esc to close the crafting screen as you would close the inventory screen.**

6. **Right-click a surface to place the chest there.**

If you right-click the storage chest, you can view an extra grid of squares that's almost as large as the inventory. Placing items into these slots stores them for safekeeping. You can also Shift-click items to sort them from the inventory into the chest, and vice versa. Always keep most of your valuables in storage when you're first starting out. As you become more comfortable playing the game, you can carry more items with you, just in case.

Do not place a block directly above a chest, or it won't open.

Placing a second chest next to the first one creates an elongated chest, which stores twice as many stacks in the same place for more efficiency.

Shelter and door

Wandering around in the open usually isn't a problem during the day, but your environment becomes much more dangerous at night. If your daytime minutes are waning and you don't feel ready to fight back (which is probably true on your first day), you need shelter. By placing many of the blocks you've gathered, you can build shelters, houses, and other structures.

As you gain experience, you can invent your own architectural strategies. To build a basic shelter for now, follow these steps:

1. **Find a good building spot.**

   Flat spots are easiest to build on, but you can find any spot that you think is feasible for a house to fit. Remember that you can break and replace dirt, sand, and other blocks to flatten a rough area.

2. **Select a block in the inventory with the 1–9 keys, and then right-click a nearby surface to place it there. Place several blocks in a comfortably sized outline for your base of operations, as shown in Figure 2-4.**

Figure 2-4: Starting your base

Usually, the frame is a rectangle made of wooden planks, but you can collect blocks such as dirt and use them for building in a pinch. You will also need a door, so you can leave one block out of your rectangle to make room for it. You can also build the rectangle around your crafting table and chest so that you can work from inside your home.

3. **Place a second layer of blocks on top of the first layer.**

   A structure that's two blocks tall is sufficient to keep most monsters at bay.

Next, craft a door so that you have a simple way to enter and exit your shelter. To build a door, use the crafting table and follow these steps:

1. **Right-click the crafting table to open the crafting grid.**

2. **Arrange six wooden planks in two adjacent columns of the crafting grid.**

   This arrangement is the recipe for a door.

3. **Move the door to the bottom row of your inventory.**

4. **Place the door in the wall of your shelter by right-clicking the ground where you want it.**

   You may have to break open part of the shelter wall to fit the door.

5. **Right-click the door to open (and close) it.**

When you place a door in front of you, the door is positioned to open away from you when you right-click it. Usually, a door is placed from the outside of a building so that it opens toward the inside.

Figure 2-5 shows a finished shelter with a door.

Figure 2-5: Crafting a door and finishing your shelter

To place a block beneath you, jump into the air while right-clicking and looking straight down. This popular method for building and scaffolding is referred to as *pillar jumping.* If you repeat this strategy, you can effectively rise upward on a pillar of blocks, which is useful for building taller structures.

That's it — generally, a basic shelter can ensure your safety for the night.

Completing Optional Day One Activities

After you've taken care of the basic tasks of creating a crafting table, chest, and house, you can move on to the truly fun activities in Minecraft: exploring, building, gathering, fighting, and engaging in other outlets of invention. This section details some useful ways you can spend the rest of your daylight minutes.

Use Chapter 4 and the online bonus chapter and appendix (available as free downloads at www.dummies.com/go/minecraftfd) for details on blocks, items, and crafting recipes.

Sticks and wooden tools

Sticks and wooden tools set you on your way to obtaining many useful items. To create sticks, open your inventory or right-click the crafting table, and put two vertically adjacent planks into the crafting grid. Four sticks are created for every two planks.

Sticks have no use on their own, but you can use them to craft a variety of other items. By arranging sticks and planks on a crafting table, you can create wooden tools. Tools are used for breaking blocks and fighting quickly and effectively, and although wooden tools break easily and work slowly, they provide a good start.

Here's a rundown of wooden tools to create (see Chapter 4 or the online appendix at www.dummies.com/go/minecraftfd for the recipes):

- **Wooden pickaxe:** You use this item to mine stone-based blocks. (If you try to break stone by hand, it takes a long time and doesn't even drop an item.) Often, a pickaxe is the only wooden tool you need. Any stone-based blocks you break while the pickaxe is selected break faster, so keep it in the bottom row of your inventory for quick access. Breaking stone blocks with a pickaxe provides cobblestone, which is used for stone-based products. (See Chapter 4 for information about the Stone age.)

- **Wooden axe:** Break wood-based blocks faster.

- **Wooden shovel:** Break granulated blocks faster, such as dirt, sand, and gravel.

- **Wooden hoe:** Till dirt or grass for farming wheat, carrots, potatoes, melons, and pumpkins. (See Chapter 5 for more on farming.)

- **Wooden sword:** Deal extra damage to enemies while this item is selected.

When you use a tool, a green bar representing *durability* appears under it; the durability slowly depletes as you continue to use the tool. Once the meter runs out, the tool breaks, and you have to craft a new one.

Cobblestone and coal

Cobblestone is a useful building and crafting material. Obtain this item by mining stone (a common, gray block, also known as *smooth stone*) with a pickaxe. You can dig to find stone or look for a cave, mountain, or crag with a visible amount of stone.

This section also covers coal, the most common ore of the game, and how to obtain and use it. Figure 2-6 shows several basic stone- and coal-based items, such as stone, cobblestone, coal, stone tools, a torch, and a furnace.

Figure 2-6: Basic stone- and coal-based items

The following list explains how to obtain these items:

✔ **Stone tools:** Crafted in the same way as wooden tools, except with cobblestone rather than wooden planks. Stone tools are faster and have twice the durability of wooden tools. Also, the stone pickaxe can mine lapis lazuli and iron ore (described in Chapter 4 and in the bonus chapter, available for download at www.dummies. com/go/minecraftfd).

✔ **Furnace:** Crafted with eight cobblestone blocks. After you right-click the furnace, a new screen appears with two input slots and an output slot; place fuel in the bottom slot and an item in the top slot to cook the item. See Chapter 4 for more details about using the furnace.

✔ **Coal:** Used to craft torches and fuel furnaces. Coal can be found by mining coal ore, commonly found underground but occasionally aboveground. You can also cook wood blocks in a furnace to get charcoal, which has the same properties.

✔ **Torch:** Can be placed on a floor or a wall as a light source. These lights are always important because darkness provides a place for monsters to spawn — and you don't want them to appear in places where you need to go. Use a stick and a lump of coal to craft four torches.

Bed

The incredibly useful bed lets you sleep through the night — bypassing all its dangers — as long as you aren't being pursued by monsters. To craft a bed, you need wool blocks, obtained by killing sheep that roam around grassy areas. Craft three of these blocks with three wooden planks to make a bed. Place the bed in your shelter and right-click it at night to sleep!

Note that these two messages may appear onscreen and prevent you from sleeping:

✔ You can only sleep at night. Wait until the sun sets a little more before trying again.

✔ You may not rest now, there are monsters nearby. You have to look for whatever creature is trying to kill you and destroy it before sleeping.

Continue working on the items in the previous sections of this chapter until nighttime. That's when the fun begins.

Preparing to Survive

Unless you set the difficulty level to Peaceful, you *will* face danger during the night. These five types of enemies appear during the night (look over the basic controls in Chapter 1, if you haven't already):

 ✓ **Creepers** are the most well-known enemies — these cute green shrub-monsters walk toward you, hiss, and explode, harming you and destroying nearby blocks. Attack while sprinting (double-tap the W key) to knock back creepers before they explode. When you play in a higher difficulty mode, creepers can kill your avatar *in one shot.*

 ✓ **Endermen** might not appear on the first night, but sooner or later, you'll see one. Don't antagonize these monsters — they can be challenging even for experienced players. Endermen normally don't attack you, but if you place the crosshair over one, it turns and glares at you, ready to attack you the moment you remove the crosshair. If you're unfortunate enough to anger this creature, watch out for its powerful attacks and teleportation. Its weaknesses are water and sunlight.

 ✓ **Skeletons** are downright tricky — they approach you tactically and fire arrows at you. Skeletons are impeccable archers, so hide behind blocks to avoid them.They shoot faster as you get closer, so sneaking up on them is your best bet.

 ✓ **Spiders** have a relatively small amount of health, but they are fast, small, and jumpy, making them difficult to hit. They can also climb walls, so be prepared to defend your shelter.

 ✓ **Zombies** are fairly easy to vanquish if you see them coming. They have more health than other enemies, but they move slowly. Don't let them stall you long enough for other monsters to notice you.

Attacks inflict more damage when you're jumping. You can tell when you score a "jump attack" by the sparks that appear on the enemy. Watch out, though: Jumping makes you hungry. (Read more about hunger in Chapter 3.)

When it's daytime again, the world becomes safer. The undead catch fire in sunlight, spiders no longer attack you, and endermen disappear as they teleport away from the harmful light; creepers are still harmful, but they eventually leave as well. Regardless of how many deaths your avatar has accumulated, you can freely say that you have survived your first night. After you complete a bit of work, and discover more about the game in other chapters, your little shelter can become a bastion of power and wealth.

3

Overcoming Long-Term Obstacles

A fter you understand the basic components of setup and safety outlined in Chapter 2, read this chapter to examine the deeper concepts of the game, grasp the basics of staying well-fed, and follow the steps for crafting your fortune and taking the fight back to the world.

Understanding and Avoiding Hunger

Hunger is a dangerous long-term obstacle — it is useful to overcome it as efficiently as possible. As depicted by the Hunger bar at the bottom of the screen, you get hungry over time and require food to resolve it. (Refer to Chapter 1 for more on the Hunger bar.)

Eating food restores your character's health indirectly over time, so keep at least 9 out of 10 units on your Hunger bar. Your symptoms of hunger depend on the difficulty level. If it is not at the Peaceful level, your character grows hungrier by taking action: Sprinting (by double-tapping W) is the easiest way to go hungry, but jumping or absorbing damage also taxes your avatar.

You cannot sprint if the Hunger bar has 3 units or fewer.

The consequence of famine (as depicted by an empty Hunger bar) depends on the current difficulty level, as outlined in Table 3-1.

Table 3-1	Effects of Famine on Your Character
Difficulty	*What Happens to the Health Bar*
Peaceful	The Health bar does not deplete.
Easy	Assuming that the Health bar is more than half full, it slowly depletes until it's half full.
Normal	It slowly depletes, but not to the point of death.
Hard	It depletes until it's empty. Find some food — quick!

To refill the Hunger bar, find sustenance, as described next.

Acquiring food

Table 3-2 lists several useful foods and explains how to obtain them. Chapter 4 has more information about the items themselves. If you're starting a new game, strive for the foods near the top of the table.

Table 3-2		Useful Foodstuffs
Icon	*Food*	*Description*
	Raw pork-chop or beef	Killing a pig or cow grants you 1 to 3 units of this food. However, the food is more effective when cooked in a furnace.
	Cooked pork-chop or steak	Cook raw meat in a furnace to obtain an item worth 4 units of food.
	Raw chicken	Avoid eating raw chicken unless you have to. Every item you eat gives you a 30 percent chance of getting food poisoning, draining the Hunger bar.
	Cooked chicken	It has the same effect as cooked pork or beef, but, at 3 units of food, is less powerful.

Icon	Food	Description
	Mushroom stew	This item restores 3 units of food, and each inventory space holds only one bowl of stew.
	Bread	Bread isn't quite as satiating as meat, but after you obtain a wheat farm (described in Chapter 5), you can craft a reliable food source, 2 ½ units in strength.
	Cookie	Cookies are crafted from wheat, but you also need cocoa beans. Restoring 1 unit of food apiece, cookies aren't very restorative, though you can mass-produce them.
	Carrot	Carrots are found incidentally when you kill zombies or explore villages (as described in Chapter 8). A carrot provides 2 units of food.
	Potato	Potatoes are also found incidentally. Raw potatoes aren't very useful, but can be cooked into baked potatoes.
	Baked potato	Cook potatoes in a furnace to get this item, worth 3 units of food.
	Melon slice	Despite the meager effect of a single slice, or 1 unit, this item can be mass-produced effectively.
	Red apple	This fruit falls from destroyed trees and provides 2 units of food.
	Golden apple	Both types of golden apple yield 2 units of food. The first, crafted with gold nuggets, boosts your health and reduces your hunger. The second, crafted with gold blocks, gives you 30 seconds of rapid regeneration and 5 minutes of resistance and fire resistance.
	Raw fish	Fishing is mentioned in Chapter 4.
	Cooked fish	Cook fish in a furnace to get this item, worth 2 ½ units of food; it makes a good food source if you have time on your hands.

(continued)

Table 3-2 *(continued)*

Icon	Food	Description
	Pumpkin pie	Collect eggs (littered by chickens), sugar (from lakeside reeds), and pumpkins to make a pie worth 4 units of food.
	Cake	Making a cake requires 3 buckets of milk, 2 lumps of sugar, 3 units of wheat, and 1 egg. Cake has to be placed on the ground before you can eat it; right-click it to restore 1 unit of food. Cake disappears after six uses.
	Rotten flesh	Eating rotten flesh — obtained from zombies — gives you an 80 percent chance of food poisoning.
	Spider eye	Eating a spider eye — obtained from spiders — has the side effect of poisoning you. The eye is used primarily for brewing potions.

Eating food

You can eat foodstuffs by selecting food and holding down the right mouse button for a second. Your avatar then finishes eating and part of the Hunger bar is refilled.

In addition to restoring the Hunger bar, eating food prevents it from depleting for a while. When the Hunger bar starts jittering, you're becoming hungry again, and the meter continues to deplete.

If you don't want to repeatedly run back to your home to eat, carry road rations with you, such as steak or bread.

Building, Mining, and Farming

If you have a source of food and a shelter (as described in Chapter 2), you're essentially safe survival-wise — which is, of course, only a small portion of the game. As you begin mining, adventuring, and upgrading, you face challenges just difficult enough to meet your personal level of caution.

Building an effective house

One creative goal in Minecraft is building. Although a wooden rectangle with a door is likely to satisfy most of your needs, having a giant house full of storage chests, farms, and other tidbits is always satisfying — and a welcome sight after completing a long adventure. Though building is primarily left to your creativity, a few tips can help you build quickly and easily:

- **To build upward,** jump and quickly place a block underneath yourself. Repeat this action to make a pillar.

- **To build off a ledge,** hold the Shift key (so that you don't fall) and walk up to the rim of the ledge. Then you can place blocks on the side of the ledge.

- **To build a floor,** move backward while placing blocks in front of you to make a line. To fill a space, repeat in any pattern you choose.

Starting on a mine or an excavation

One vital activity in Minecraft is mining, because you obtain the minerals necessary to expand your selection of resources. You can start a mine by digging or by finding a cave — both methods are detailed in Chapter 5. For now, obtain or craft the following items before you start mining (you can find recipes for these items in Chapter 4 and the appendix, available for download at www.dummies.com/go/minecraftfd):

- **Pickaxe:** Most underground blocks are difficult to break — and require a pickaxe. Though stone pickaxes usually work well, iron pickaxes are necessary to harvest higher-level minerals. You can find iron while mining.

- **Torch:** As you descend into the ground and away from sunlight, nighttime monsters become even more dangerous. Especially when you're in a cave, bring several torches with you and conquer the dangerous den by lighting the dark areas. Lighting your way is always useful because most monsters don't appear in light.

- **Food:** Always take food with you on a long mining trip. If you get lost, it buys you some time to dig your way out.

The most important resource you must look for underground is ore. Minecraft has seven types of ore, described in Table 3-3.

Table 3-3		The Ores
Icon	*Name*	*Description*
	Coal ore	Break it with any pickaxe. This block drops a lump of coal when broken, which is useful for crafting and smelting.
	Diamond ore	Use a pickaxe made of iron or diamond. Diamond is the strongest material that can be crafted into tools. Diamond is also used to build such powerful items as enchanting tables.
	Emerald ore	Use a pickaxe made of iron or diamond. This incidental ore, found only underneath hills, drops emeralds that can be used when trading with villagers. (See Chapter 8 for information about trading.)
	Gold ore	Use a pickaxe made of iron or diamond. Cook this block in a furnace to get gold ingots. Gold is used for more miscellaneous items.
	Iron ore	Use a pickaxe made of stone, iron, or diamond. You must cook this block in a furnace to obtain iron ingots.
	Lapis lazuli ore	Use a pickaxe made of stone, iron, or diamond. Lapis ore can be broken into 4 to 8 lumps of lapis lazuli. Lapis is used for blue dye, or you can craft it into lapis lazuli blocks for decoration.
	Redstone ore	Use a pickaxe made of iron or diamond. This special ore lights up when touched. You can break it to obtain four or five lumps of redstone dust, which is used for potions and mechanisms (as described in Chapter 6).

As you start mining, you can obtain the cobblestone and ores necessary to craft more tools and items. Obtaining an abundance of powerful ores is an important long-term goal in Minecraft.

Starting a farm

If you don't like the concept of starting a farm and waiting impatiently for crops to grow, don't be turned off by this section's heading. In Minecraft, *farm* generally refers to a system that produces resources without your active participation. Fortunately, most farms take only a short time to produce resources, and Minecraft has plenty of content to keep you busy while you wait for a farm to flourish. Using blocks and items creatively allows for many different types of farms. Basic types of farms are detailed in Chapter 5, but you can find more inventive strategies for farming items in Chapter 6.

Advancing Toward the End

As you pursue your own, open-ended goals, track your accomplishments by advancing through the steps of the game. The loosely structured advancement system in Minecraft provides guidelines for growing and prospering in the world. Use this section as a guide to finding your next major goal in Minecraft. Even experienced players can take a while to complete these goals.

Obtaining better ores

The first step in becoming more powerful is to advance past the Stone Age. As detailed in the earlier section "Starting on a mine or an excavation," you can go mining to find better materials such as iron and diamond. By using the crafting recipes in the bonus chapter and appendix (both available for download at www.dummies.com/go/minecraftfd), you can build stronger weapons, tools, armor, and utility items. Obtain as much iron as you can, and use it to stock up on gold, redstone, and diamond.

Reaching the Nether

A major step in Minecraft is building the portal that transports you from the classic overworld into the *Nether* dimension — a dangerous place with an interesting new set of blocks and monsters. To unlock more items — and reach the next stage of the game — you have to reach the Nether.

Building a portal

Building your first nether portal requires a source of water and lava, as well as a flint and an iron ingot. Follow these general steps to build one, as shown in Figure 3-1:

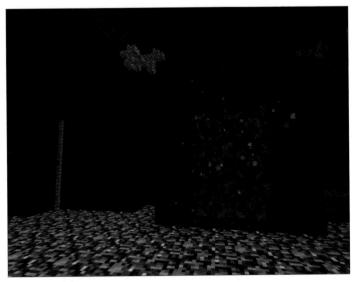

Figure 3-1: The Nether and its portal

1. **Get at least ten obsidian blocks, which are formed by pouring water over still lava.**

   The incredibly hard block of *obsidian* is breakable only by a diamond pickaxe. To mix some obsidian:

   a. Craft a bucket by using iron ingots.

   b. Right-click water or lava to pick it up.

   c. Right-click to replace a liquid; place both liquids on top of each other to make obsidian.

   d. Mine the obsidian with a diamond pickaxe or simply mix it directly into the frame (detailed in Step 2).

2. **Build an obsidian frame that encloses a rectangle two blocks wide and three blocks high.**

   This step requires 14 obsidian blocks (or 10, if you skip the corners).

3. Light the interior.

Now, you have only a hollow black rectangle. To turn it into a portal, you give the interior a little spark. The easiest way to do so is to craft flint and steel from an iron ingot and a flint (sometimes dropped from gravel blocks). Right-clicking surfaces with flint and steel lights them on fire, but reduces the lighter's durability. Right-click the interior of the frame with the flint and steel to fill it with purple smoke. This smoke is a portal to the Nether.

To use the portal, stand inside the frame until the screen fades into purple. You will soon appear in the Nether next to a second portal that can take you home.

Surviving the Nether

The *Nether* is a huge, cave-like landscape made mostly of netherrack, a weak reddish stone. *Soul sand*, a block that slows your avatar, is found in large patches along with gravel. The floor of the Nether is covered in a huge lava lake, and the ceiling contains shining stalactites made of glowstone.

During your visit to the Nether, try to find a nether fortress — which is a giant structure, made of red bricks, that resembles a broken castle. Powerful enemies appear in the fortress, but these enemies are also your key to the Stronghold, the next stage of the game.

This list describes enemies you may confront in the Nether:

✔ **Zombie pigman:** Despite its frightening appearance, this creature wants nothing to do with you. If you attack one, however, every other zombie pigman in sight will rush toward you, inflicting a considerable amount of damage with their swords. Killing a zombie pigman yields rotten flesh, gold nuggets, and occasionally, other gold items.

How to fight it: Ensure that the group cannot surround or corner you, and try to defeat them one at a time.

✔ **Ghast:** This airborne, white jellyfish is dangerous. It tries to elude you while spitting explosive fireballs. A single battle with a ghast can turn a patch of netherrack into a burning wasteland.

How to fight it: Attack its tentacles with a bow and arrow, or hit the fireballs to reflect them back at the ghast. Also note that ghasts cannot destroy hard blocks like cobblestone.

 ✔ **Magma cube:** This fiery, red cube hops after you, inflicting damage on impact. Step back after killing a large one — it splits into smaller magma cubes. Only tiny cubes drop items, and they provide *magma cream,* which is used in brewing potions.

How to fight it: Attack it right after it jumps to outmaneuver it.

 ✔ **Wither skeleton:** This darker version of the skeletons outside the Nether patrol nether fortresses with their stone swords. Don't let one of them reach you! Its sword causes you to *wither* for a short time, which slowly drains the Health bar and (unlike poison) potentially kills your avatar. This type of skeleton is occasionally backed up by common skeleton archers (as described in Chapter 7).

How to fight it: Because it appears mostly in nether fortresses, make sure you fight it in a long passage where it can't corner you. A bow and arrow work very well.

 ✔ **Blaze:** This floating, fiery construct surrounds the watchtowers of the nether fortress. The watchtowers have burning, metal grates that constantly create new Blaze. You can break this spawner with a pickaxe, but you need Blaze in order to obtain certain items. When a Blaze begins to emit fire, it is preparing to throw a triple-fireball attack that's incredibly dangerous. Upon death, it drops useful blaze rods.

How to fight them: Kill Blaze as fast as possible and don't let them trap you under heavy fire. You can hurt Blaze by throwing snowballs at them! You can also resist them using fire resistance potions (as mentioned in Chapter 6).

Finding the Stronghold

After you're familiar with the Nether (and, possibly, you've worked on your house and mine), it's time to head toward the *Stronghold.* This huge, underground structure appears in the overworld and contains the end portal — the passage to the final dimension.

Unfortunately, the Stronghold is generally difficult to find — you need resources from the Nether to detect it. Follow these steps to find the Stronghold:

1. **Collect ender pearls.**

   These items are dropped by endermen (see Chapter 7). You may have to explore a bit during the night to find some. It's hard to tell how many ender pearls you need, so collect a few and follow these steps, and then go back for more pearls if you don't have enough.

2. **Collect blaze powder.**

   Kill some Blaze in the Nether to obtain blaze rods, which can be crafted into powder. (For the recipe, see the appendix at www.dummies.com/go/minecraftfd.) You need at least as much blaze powder as ender pearls.

3. **Craft the blaze powder and ender pearls into eyes of ender.**

   Place one of each in the crafting grid in any order.

4. **Select an eye of ender and then right-click to throw it.**

   The eye of ender drifts into the sky, angled in the direction of the Stronghold. If the eye moves forward, for example, the Stronghold lies ahead.

5. **Follow the eye of ender to move toward the Stronghold. Continue to throw eyes until they begin floating down instead of up.**

   After the eye of ender has hovered for a while, it either drops back down to be used again or shatters. Craft several eyes and follow them toward the Stronghold.

6. **When the eyes begin floating down, dig to find the Stronghold.**

After you reach the Stronghold, you fall into a ruined stone chamber with a white-and-green frame in the center. The room also contains a fiery grating that spawns silverfish (a giant bug described in Chapter 7). Use a pickaxe to break this grating and then approach the green frame. (It would contain the end portal, but it's broken.) To repair and activate the end portal, use 12 more eyes of ender to fill in each empty slot in the frame, as shown in Figure 3-2.

Figure 3-2: End portal

Conquering the End

Don't jump into the end portal just yet — you face a battle when you enter, and you must be prepared. Explore the Stronghold and find items in treasure chests. Get a sword, a bow with sufficient ammunition, and some blocks. Also, take safety precautions, by placing a storage chest and bed near the portal.

 Drop off any unnecessary valuables before entering the End so that you don't lose them, and don't be afraid to delay your entry for a while.

When you're ready, you can jump into the portal. You're immediately transported to the *End* — a dimension, smaller than the Nether, that consists of a few floating platforms, as shown in Figure 3-3.

You immediately notice these elements of the End:

✔ **Endermen:** The place is full of these creatures, as mentioned in Chapter 2. You don't want a swarm of them on your heels, so don't look at any of them — an enderman will attack you if your crosshair passes over it.

 If you can't seem to avoid looking at endermen, place a pumpkin in the Helmet slot of your inventory. You can wear the pumpkin on your head like a Halloween mask! It makes seeing difficult, but also lets you look at endermen without angering them.

Figure 3-3: The End

⮑ **Ender dragon:** If the dragon is nearby, the *Boss Health bar* appears at the top of the screen to represent the ender dragon. This huge, black dragon flies around the stage and tries to run you down.

⮑ **Pillars:** Many obsidian pillars dot the End, and each one holds a crystal. If you cause damage to the ender dragon, it can fly to a crystal and heal itself. You have to destroy these crystals to bring down the dragon.

To defeat the dragon, consider these suggestions:

⮑ **Destroy the ender prisms.** These vulnerable crystals explode when touched. You can destroy most of them by hitting them with arrows, snowballs, or eggs. If you simply can't reach one, use blocks to *pillar-jump* (jump and place a block under you) until you reach the top of the pillar. Be careful when smashing the prism: The explosion causes damage and may knock you off the pillar.

Keep an eye on the dragon — it can inflict a lot of damage if it charges you. It destroys any block it touches except for the ones appearing in the End. Turn away the dragon by attacking it.

⮑ **Attack the ender dragon.** The rest of the fight is fairly straightforward. When the dragon charges you, attack it with everything you have. Shoot arrows at it if you want, and don't worry about the arrows hitting any endermen — they teleport to avoid the projectile and don't pursue you.

After the ender dragon is defeated, it slowly drifts into the air, where it breaks apart and explodes in a shower of experience orbs. Collect as many as you can! The dragon also drops a gray fountain with an egg on top. The egg is decorative, teleporting when you right-click it. Jump into the black depths of the fountain to view a cutscene and then return to the overworld.

Staying busy in the afterglow

The End is somewhat of a misnomer — even after you beat the dragon and leave the End, the game is far from over. You have the orbs necessary to perform powerful enchantments (detailed in Chapter 6), and the End provides a good source of obsidian and ender pearls. Your house and resources are still there — now it's time to fulfill your own goals. Build giant castles, collect loads of diamonds, craft new items, and explore. You can also fight the wither, an optional boss detailed in Chapter 7.

4

Discovering Blocks and Implementing Items

In This Chapter

▶ Exploring the Wooden, Looting, and Stone ages

▶ Finding detailed information about blocks and items

▶ Using the furnace

*T*his chapter is a guide to the basic components of Survival mode that you need to know when you're just starting out. This chapter includes information on the Wooden, Looting, and Stone ages, as well as details on how to use the furnace.

If you're interested in finding out more detailed information about other blocks and items, be sure to check out the bonus chapter; and for images and detailed crafting recipes, check out the bonus appendix. (Both the bonus chapter and appendix are available for download at www.dummies.com/go/minecraftfd.)

The Wooden Age

When you first start playing Minecraft, most of the items you need are wooden. Table 4-1 explains how to find or craft these items and describes what they do. You can break most of these blocks faster with an axe.

Table 4-1   **Wooden Items**

Item	How to Obtain It	Description
Boat	Crafted from 5 planks	Right-click some water in which to put your boat, and then right-click the boat to hop in! Press the W,A,S,D keys to drive, and inflict damage on the boat to break it and use it again later.
Bowl	Crafted from 3 planks (makes 4)	The bowl holds mushroom stew.
Chest	Crafted from 8 planks	The storage unit can hold 27 stacks of items. Place two chests next to each other to form a double chest, which can store 54 stacks.
Crafting table	Crafted from 4 planks	Right-click this item to open the expanded crafting grid (see Chapter 2).
Fence	Crafted from 6 sticks (makes 2)	Its posts are decorative blocks that automatically connect to adjacent blocks or fences. Though you can still place blocks on top of fences, you cannot jump over them.
Fence gate	Crafted from 2 planks, 4 sticks	Click to open and close its sideways latch. It connects to, and acts like, fences.
Ladder	Crafted from 7 sticks (makes 3)	Ladders can be placed on walls, and you can climb ladders by simply moving toward them. Hold the Shift key to hang on a ladder.
Log	Found on trees	Wooden logs come in four textures, used for crafting. You can place logs on walls to make them appear sideways.
Sign	Crafted from 6 planks, 1 stick (makes 3)	When you place this item on a wall, or at any angle on the ground, a screen appears on which you can write.
Stick	Crafted from 2 planks (makes 4)	Make it with wooden planks for more crafting recipes.
Trap door	Crafted from 6 planks (makes 2)	Place this hatch on the side of a block. Click the hatch to open or close it.

Item	How to Obtain It	Description
Wooden axe	Crafted from 2 sticks, 3 planks	A weak axe, it makes lumberjacking somewhat quicker.
Wooden button	Crafted from 1 plank	This simple item provides power when you click it or hit it with an arrow (see Chapter 6).
Wooden door	Crafted from 6 planks	This tall block can be opened and closed when you click it. Zombies can destroy it (see Chapter 8).
Wooden hoe	Crafted from 2 sticks, 2 planks	The easily broken garden tool is helpful for starting a small farm at a low cost.
Wooden pickaxe	Crafted from 2 sticks, 3 planks	This weak pickaxe is the most basic tool for breaking stone blocks. It's your ticket to the next age.
Wooden plank	Crafted from 1 log (makes 4)	This basis for wooden items is a useful building material. Its texture depends on which logs were used to make it.
Wooden pressure plate	Crafted from 2 planks	It provides power when anything lands on it (see Chapter 6).
Wooden shovel	Crafted from 2 sticks, 1 plank	The weakest shovel in the game is a cheap one.
Wooden slab	Crafted from 3 planks (makes 6)	Walk up and down this decorative block without jumping. Stack the slabs on top of each other, and place them as either ceilings or floors.
Wooden stair	Crafted from 6 planks (makes 4)	The wooden stair allows for denser stairwells and can be placed upside-down on ceilings, like the slab.

Note: Stairs are always placed facing you. |
| Wooden sword | Crafted from 1 stick, 2 planks | A brittle, basic sword that increases the damage you inflict, it's a good go-to weapon for new players. |

Of course, you may come across many other natural blocks during the Wooden Age. Table 4-2 lists the common above-ground blocks and describes the items you can make with them.

Table 4-2   Basic Naturals from the Wooden Age

Item	How to Obtain It	Description
Apple	Occasionally, from oak leaves	A food item that can be used to make golden apples
Cacti	Found in deserts	A farmable plant (see Chapter 5) that damages anything that touches it; can be made into green dye
Clay ball	By breaking clay blocks (4 per block)	Used to make bricks and clay blocks
Clay block	Found near water	A softly colored building block; drops 4 clay balls when broken
Cocoa bean	Occasionally, from natural cocoa pods in the jungle	Used as brown dye or to make cookies; can also be farmed (see Chapter 5)
Dead shrub	Found in deserts	Used as decoration
Dirt	Found in most biomes, usually with grass on top	Can be used as farmland; nearby grass eventually spreads onto dirt
Flint	While mining gravel	Used for crafting flint and steel, or arrows
Flower	Found in grassy biomes	Can be picked up and replanted or crafted into dyes
Grass, dead bush, fern	Found in grassy biomes	A grass that can be grown manually using bone meal; sometimes drops seeds when broken without shears
Gravel	Found randomly aboveground and below it	Falls if no block is under it; sometimes drops flint
Ice	Found on the surface of frozen lakes and rivers	A slippery block that commonly appears in bodies of water that have frozen over
Leaf	Found on trees	Unless you break it with shears, drops only saplings or apples
Lily pad	Found in swamp biomes	Can be placed on water, allowing you to walk across it with ease

Item	How to Obtain It	Description
Mushroom	Found in dark places or swamps or near trees	Can be used to make stew, but cannot be placed in bright areas
Mushroom stew	Crafted from 1 brown mushroom, 1 red mushroom, 1 bowl	A useful food item, though only one bowl fits in an inventory slot
Paper	Crafted from 3 sugar canes (makes 3)	Used to make maps and books; purchased by librarians for emeralds (see Chapter 8)
Pumpkin	Appears occasionally in patches	A fruit that can be farmed (see Chapter 5), converted to a jack-o'-lantern, used to build golems, crafted into seeds, or made into pie
Pumpkin seed	Crafted from 1 pumpkin (makes 4)	Used to farm pumpkins; see Chapter 5
Sand	Found in deserts and around bodies of water	Falls if no block is under it; can be used to make sandstone or glass
Sapling	From leaf blocks	Planted when you right-click grass or dirt; grows into a tree (see Chapter 5)
Snow	Appears in snowy biomes	A thin layer of snow over cold biomes that can be scooped up into snowballs
Snow block	Crafted from 4 snowballs	A decoration block that can be used to build snow golems
Snowball	Appears when shoveling snow	Can be thrown to knock back mobs and deal damage to Blaze and the ender dragon; can be crafted into snow blocks
Sugar	Crafted from 1 sugar cane	Used to brew potions and to make fermented spider eyes, pumpkin pie, and cake
Sugar cane	Appears in patches near water	A reed that can be farmed (see Chapter 5) and crafted into paper or sugar
Vine	Appears on trees in swamps and in jungles	Can be climbed; grows if left untended; if hanging, disappears if its roots are destroyed

The Looting Age

You reach the Looting Age early in the game — sometimes, even parallel to reaching the Wooden Age. You begin by slaying enemies for loot, and by using the loot to improve your crafting repertoire. Many more items then become available to you, as listed in Table 4-3. I don't mention some rare loot like iron in this section; these items are described in their respective tables.

All tools increase the amount of damage you inflict. The sword and bow are the most powerful, but an axe still fares well in combat. Shovels are the weakest.

Table 4-3		Items in the Looting Age
Item	*How to Obtain It*	*Description*
Arrow	By killing skeletons; crafted from 1 flint, 1 stick, 1 feather (makes 4)	A type of ammunition used with bows and dispensers
Bed	Crafted from 3 wool, 3 planks	Can be right-clicked during nighttime to sleep, skipping the night and allowing you to reappear by your bed if you die
		(You cannot sleep while monsters are pursuing you.)
Bone	By killing skeletons	A useful item for taming wolves; can be crafted into bone meal or white dye
Bone meal	Crafted from 1 bone (makes 3)	Can right-click grass while holding this strong fertilizer to grow a patch of tall grass and flowers
		(Right-click any immature crop to grow it.)
Book	Crafted from 1 leather, 3 paper	Can be used to make a book and quill, a bookcase, or an enchantment table

Item	How to Obtain It	Description
Book and quill	Crafted from 1 feather, 1 ink sac, 1 book	Lets you write in the book or read a signed book by right-clicking while holding it
Bookshelf	Crafted from 3 books, 6 planks	An expensive decorative item that serves as a buffer for the enchantment table (see Chapter 6); it returns three books when broken
Bow	Crafted from 3 string, 3 sticks	A powerful weapon that's useful throughout the game (As long as you have arrows in your inventory, you can hold the right mouse button to charge your bow, and release it to fire.)
Carrot	Rarely, by killing zombies	Can be eaten or farmed (see Chapter 5); also used to make golden carrots
Egg	Occasionally laid by chickens	Thrown when you right-click while holding it, occasionally spawning a baby chicken where it lands; also used to craft cake and pumpkin pie
Ender pearl	Sometimes, by killing endermen	An ingredient for an eye of ender, which helps you find the Stronghold (see Chapter 3); if you throw the pearl by right-clicking, your avatar teleports to where the pearl lands, but it incurs damage
Feather	By killing chickens	A useful ingredient for arrows; also used to make the book and quill
Fermented spider eye	Crafted from 1 spider eye, 1 sugar, 1 brown mushroom	The key ingredient in negative potions (see Chapter 6)
Fishing rod	Crafted from 2 string, 3 sticks	Lets you cast its bobber by right-clicking while holding it; can be right-clicked again — if the bobber floats in the water for a little while and then suddenly dips — to pull out a fish

(continued)

Table 4-3 *(continued)*

Item	How to Obtain It	Description
Gunpowder	By killing creepers (without exploding them)	An explosive material used to craft TNT, fire charges, and splash potions
Ink sac	By killing squids	Used as black dye or as an ingredient for the book and quill
Item frame	Crafted from 8 sticks, 1 leather	Can display an item (when mounted on the wall) when you right-click it while holding the item; rotates when you right-click it again
Leather	By killing cows	Useful for making books and leather armor
Leather cap, tunic, trousers, boots	Crafted from 5, 8, 7, or 4 leather, respectively	The weakest armor that negates a good amount of damage
Painting	Crafted from 8 sticks, 1 wool	Can be placed by right-clicking a wall; measures up to 4 blocks wide by 4 blocks tall
Poisonous potato	Obtained (rarely) instead of a normal potato	Can be eaten but causes poison damage; no real use for it
Potato	Rarely, by killing zombies	Can be eaten or farmed (see Chapter 5); a low-profit food item unless cooked into a baked potato
Pumpkin pie	Crafted from 1 pumpkin, 1 sugar, 1 egg	An effective food item — reliable if you have several pumpkins and eggs
Raw beef	By killing cows	Essentially the same as raw porkchop
Raw chicken	By killing chickens	A weaker food source that can sometimes poison you when eaten raw, draining your food meter; should be cooked before eating!

Item	How to Obtain It	Description
Raw fish	Obtained by fishing	Restores a tiny segment of the Hunger bar and can be used to tame ocelots in the jungle
Raw porkchop	By killing pigs	A basic food item that isn't effective unless you cook it
Rotten flesh	By killing zombies	A fairly useless item and volatile food source; however, heals wolves when fed to them; sometimes, village priests exchange an emerald for it (see Chapter 8)
Slimeball	Dropped by slimes in the swamp	A gooey item, used to make sticky pistons and magma cream
Spider eye	By killing spiders	A potion ingredient, a poisonous food, and an ingredient of a fermented spider eye
String	By killing spiders	A useful ingredient in making bows, fishing rods, and tripwire lines
TNT	Crafted from 5 gunpowder, 4 sand	When set off by redstone or fire, sizzles and then causes a large block-destroying explosion; affected by gravity when activated
Wool	By killing or shearing sheep; crafted from 4 string	A decorative block used for beds and paintings; can be colored with dye

The Stone Age

A significant milestone in Minecraft Survival mode, and one achieved by some players on the first day, is reaching the Stone Age. After you craft a wooden pickaxe and you either find a cave or dig a hole, the items in Table 4-4 become available to you.

Most stone-based materials are more solid than other blocks, and you have to break them with a pickaxe to obtain loot.

Table 4-4   **Items in the Stone Age**

Item	How to Obtain It	Description
Coal	Found when mining coal ore; dropped by wither skeletons	A handy material that's used as furnace fuel; can be used to make torches and fire charges
Coal ore	Found commonly underground	A plentiful source of coal that you can find in veins while mining
Cobblestone	Found by mining stone or cobblestone	An excellent building block and the basis for stone-based crafting
Cobblestone slab	Crafted from 3 cobblestone (makes 6)	The cobblestone equivalent of the wooden slab
Cobblestone stairs	Crafted from 6 cobblestone (makes 4)	The cobblestone equivalent of wooden stairs
Cobblestone wall	Crafted from 6 cobblestone (makes 6)	The cobblestone equivalent of wooden fences; connects to fence gates
Furnace	Crafted from 8 cobblestone	A useful block that's used to smelt items into other items
Jack-o'-lantern	Crafted from 1 pumpkin, 1 torch	A spooky, brightly glowing pumpkin
Lever	Crafted from 1 cobblestone, 1 stick	A power source that can be turned on and off by right-clicking; see Chapter 6
Sandstone	Appears underground in the desert and in desert structures; crafted from 4 sand	The "stone" version of sand; can occur naturally or artificially
Sandstone slab	Crafted from 3 sandstone (makes 6)	The sandstone equivalent of the wooden slab
Sandstone stairs	Crafted from 6 sandstone (makes 4)	The sandstone equivalent of the wooden stairs
Smooth, chiseled sandstone	Crafted from 2 sandstone slabs for chiseled, or 4 sandstone (makes 4) for smooth	A decoration block

Item	How to Obtain It	Description
Stone axe	Crafted from 3 cobblestone, 2 sticks	A tool that chops wooden blocks much faster than normal
Stone hoe	Crafted from 2 cobblestone, 2 sticks	As efficient as a wooden hoe, but with more durability
Stone pickaxe	Crafted from 3 cobblestone, 2 sticks	A more durable pickaxe, capable of mining more blocks
Stone shovel	Crafted from 1 cobblestone, 2 sticks	A tool for digging quickly; can be used to level out dirt, gravel, sand, and other types of soft blocks
Stone sword	Crafted from 2 cobblestone, 1 stick	A strong, reliable blade that deals a moderate amount of damage
Torch	Crafted from 1 coal, 1 stick (makes 4)	A common, helpful, and cheap way to light up areas

Using the Furnace

You use the furnace, an important part of the Stone Age, to craft many more items. Placing a furnace on a surface and right-clicking it opens a menu with three slots: fuel, input, and output, as shown in Figure 4-1.

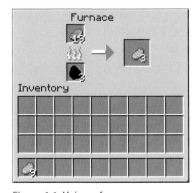

Figure 4-1: Using a furnace.

The fuel slot can take coal (eight uses per lump), wooden objects (three uses per 2 planks), and items such as blaze rods or lava buckets. It also takes a variety of other flammable items. Using a furnace grants experience orbs, and the items described in Table 4-5 become available.

Table 4-5	Furnace Items	
Item	*How to Obtain It*	*Description*
Baked potato	By cooking a potato in a furnace	A moderately effective food item
Brick	By cooking clay balls in a furnace	A simple ingredient for clay pots and brick blocks
Brick block	Crafted from 4 bricks	A dusty, red building block
Brick slab	Crafted from 3 bricks (makes 6)	The brick equivalent of the slab
Brick stairs	Crafted from 6 brick blocks (makes 4)	The brick equivalent of the stairs
Cactus green	By cooking cactus in a furnace	Used as green dye
Charcoal	By cooking wood (logs, not planks) in a furnace	Can be used for fuel, torches, and fire charges just like coal
Cooked chicken	By cooking raw chicken in a furnace	A food item, slightly less effective than pork or steak
Cooked fish	By cooking raw fish in a furnace	A food item that's easy to obtain, but not effective
Cooked porkchop or steak	By cooking raw pork or beef in a furnace	An effective food item
Flower pot	Crafted from 3 bricks	Can be placed on blocks and filled with any plant
Glass	By cooking sand in a furnace	Lets sunlight shine through windows
Glass bottle	Crafted from 3 glass (makes 3)	Fill with water to start brewing potions
Glass pane	Crafted from 6 glass (makes 16)	A thin window material that connects to adjacent blocks

Item	How to Obtain It	Description
Stone	By cooking cobblestone in a furnace	A smooth, gray block commonly located underground; restored to its smooth (from cobblestone) state by using a furnace
Stone brick	Found in the stronghold; crafted from 4 stone (makes 4)	A refined, popular decoration block
Stone brick slab	Crafted from 3 stone bricks (makes 6)	The stone brick version of the slab
Stone brick stairs	Crafted from 6 stone bricks (makes 4)	The stone brick version of the stairs
Stone button	Crafted from 1 stone	A power source that activates for a few seconds when pressed (see Chapter 6)
Stone pressure plate	Crafted from 2 stone	A power source that activates when a heavy mob steps on it (see Chapter 6)
Stone slab	Crafted from 3 stone (makes 6)	A smoother version of the cobblestone slab
Water bottle	By right-clicking a water source or full cauldron while holding a water bottle	The base ingredient for brewing potions (see Chapter 6)

5
Mastering Mines and Farms

- -

In This Chapter

▶ Taking a look at different types of mining

▶ Starting a farm

▶ Collecting various crops

- -

*W*hen you want something more strategic than simply crafting blocks and items, this chapter shows you some basic techniques for mining ores and farming various natural items.

Mining Efficiently

Mining is an incredibly useful practice that gives you a fast (though challenging) means of obtaining strong minerals such as iron, redstone, and diamond. You can mine in a number of ways, as described in this section, so use whichever method suits you best.

These mining tips aren't strict guidelines. Try your own methods, too.

Cave mining

Cave mining is challenging yet fruitful. To start, you must find a large cave — perhaps while working on another mine or exploring. If you can find a large cave, you have a useful resource at your disposal.

REMEMBER

Caves are generally *very* dark — and in Minecraft, darkness means monsters! Always be on your guard, carry weapons (and perhaps armor), and light up the cave with torches, as shown in Figure 5-1.

Figure 5-1: Lighting your way in a cave adventure

Cave mining is useful — you can obtain many scattered resources without wearing out your tools trying to plow through stone. However, caves can sometimes be deadly labyrinths, and you may lose your items if your avatar dies. You have to decide whether the payoff in resources is worth the risk of losing them.

Cave mining tips

When mining in a cave, simply light the way and skim the walls for minerals you can use. Iron ore (described in detail in the bonus chapter, available for download at www.dummies.com/go/minecraftfd) is common, but keep an eye out for it to collect it, anyway.

If you can mine deep enough, you may find useful materials such as redstone, gold, and diamond. However, you may also come across lava — the bane of careless miners. Lava flows slowly and destroys items (and you!), so avoid it and ensure that your precious ores don't fall anywhere near it.

Ravines and canyons

Sometimes, while exploring or mining, you come across *ravines*. These narrow, deep gaps can appear underground or on the surface. Although ravines can contain lots of lava and monsters and are cumbersome to navigate, they expose a lot of surface area and are useful for finding minerals.

If you enjoy mining and spend most of your time using a pick-axe, build a little rest area underground. Your house doesn't have to be located on grass.

Branch mining

If you're new to Minecraft and you don't yet have the weaponry necessary to brave a cavern, branch-mining is an effective way to obtain lots of stone and minerals. Follow these steps to dig a branch mine:

1. **Dig your way underground.**

   Dig any way you want, or see the later section "Staircase mining."

   Do not dig straight down; you might fall into a pit, or into lava.

   At the bottom of every world is a layer of unbreakable *bedrock*. Statistics have proven that ores in Minecraft are most commonly located only a few blocks above this layer, so dig until your character's y-coordinate is 13 or so. (Press F3 to see this value.)

2. **Dig a tunnel.**

   The smallest tunnel that your character can fit into is one block wide and two blocks tall. Use torches to light the area, or else your tunnel will attract unwanted guests.

3. **Build more tunnels that branch off from the first one.**

   By building extra tunnels that split off from the main route, you can look for ores over a large area. Position the tunnels two blocks apart to be able to inspect a large surface area and not miss anything (see Figure 5-2).

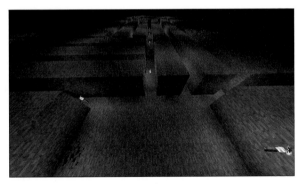

Figure 5-2: Checking a large surface area

Branch mining is effective because you can acquire a lot of ores efficiently. However, this type of mining consumes many tools because of the volume of stone you dig through, and produces much more cobblestone than valuables. Branch mining is a helpful method if you have patience, and a project in which you can invest your fortune of cobblestone.

Staircase mining

In the staircase method, you dig deeply and quickly to search for caves, find a suitable spot for a branch mine, search for minerals en route to destinations, or simply build an attractive staircase.

Descend only one block at a time, or else you can't get back up. Figure 5-3 shows a staircase, which requires a minimal amount of work.

Figure 5-3: Descending a staircase in a mine

Craft stair blocks (wooden stairs, cobblestone stairs, and others are described in Chapter 4 and in the bonus chapter, available for download at www.dummies.com/go/minecraftfd) to make the staircase's ascension less taxing. As Chapter 3 specifies, your character becomes hungry when jumping. Raise the ceiling of your staircase to make descent faster and less cramped.

Quarry mining

A *quarry* is the simplest type of mining, and digging one is a useful way to gather lots of cobblestone — and to ensure that you don't miss any materials. Simply dig a rectangle out of the ground, and then another one under it, and so on, until you have a sizeable hole from which you've unearthed every possible resource. Build a stairwell or ladder to exit and reenter the quarry. Figure 5-4 shows a classic quarry.

Figure 5-4: A classic quarry, with vines for ascending and descending

Although quarries produce lots of materials and can be mined safely, digging one requires great patience and generally isn't advisable. However, if you take that route, you can easily repurpose quarries into underground buildings.

Building the Perfect Farm

Though farming is not a required task in Minecraft, having a reliable source of renewable resources is useful. Many different items (plants, mostly) can be farmed in Minecraft, as detailed in this section.

Crops

Harvestable items such as wheat, melons, and pumpkins fit the raw definition of Minecraft farming by requiring well-irrigated farmland. Follow these general steps to set up a farm:

1. **Find a well-lit area made of grass or dirt.**

   If the area isn't well-lit, craft some torches. A flat workspace makes your task easier, though it isn't mandatory.

2. **Craft a gardening hoe (as described in Chapter 4) and use it.**

   You can right-click the ground to use the hoe to till farmland.

3. **Locate a water source nearby and then right-click it while holding a bucket. Right-click again while holding the full bucket to dump the water near your crops.**

   Dig an irrigated hole or canal in your future farm, allowing any nearby farmland to thrive. Dry farmland grows more slowly and wears out after too much time passes without crops being planted on it.

   (You can find the recipe for a bucket in the appendix, which is available for download at www.dummies. com/go/minecraftfd.)

4. **Lock up your farm.**

   Jumping on farmland destroys it. Keep crops safe from animals by building walls around the crops. Fences and fence gates work well.

After these steps are finished, you're ready to harvest crops!

Wheat, carrots, and potatoes

Wheat, carrots, and potatoes are relatively simple to farm. Simply follow these steps:

1. **Collect seeds and vegetables.**

   Breaking tall grass blocks or tilling grass blocks sometimes provides wheat seeds. You can find carrots and potatoes in villages or by killing zombies.

2. **Right-click the farmland to plant seeds, carrots, or potatoes.**

   Tiny, green stems appear on the block.

3. **Wait until the crops are fully grown.**

   Wheat is mostly yellow and brown when it's fully grown, and carrots and potatoes are ready to harvest when the heads of the vegetables begin to emerge. Work on other tasks while you wait. You can also use bone meal (crafted from skeleton bones) to grow crops instantly.

4. **Break the crop blocks to obtain your profit.**

   Replant seeds, carrots, and potatoes until your farmland is refilled, and keep the remainder as profit. Figure 5-5 shows a thriving farm.

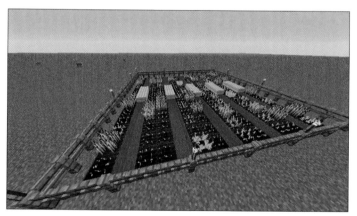

Figure 5-5: Growing crops

Using this strategy, you can start a farm that obtains items for you while you go out and enjoy the game.

Melons and pumpkins

Growing large plants such as melons and pumpkins takes quite a bit of work. Follow these steps to start a farm similar to the one in Figure 5-6:

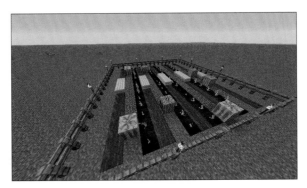

Figure 5-6: Growing melons and pumpkins

1. **Collect seeds.**

   You can find both melon and pumpkin seeds in treasure chests hidden in abandoned mineshafts. In addition, naturally found pumpkins can be crafted into seeds. Melon seeds can be crafted from melon slices, which you can get by trading with villagers, as described in Chapter 8.

2. **Right-click the farmland to plant seeds.**

   Unlike wheat, this farmland has to be adjacent to grass or dirt. When these seeds grow into stalks, they tip over and grow melons or pumpkins next to them. To grow lots of melons or pumpkins, till a row of farmland next to a row of dirt, with water pools spaced throughout.

3. **Wait.**

   Using bone meal on seeds speeds them into mature stalks, though they don't yet bear fruit. Pumpkins and melons take a while to grow. Ensure that these crops have growing space, and work on other tasks in the meantime.

4. **Harvest the crops.**

   Don't break the stalk blocks — instead, break the pumpkin and melon blocks that appear nearby. If you've grown pumpkins, you can craft them into pumpkin seeds to expand your farm. If you've grown melons, breaking the blocks produces melon slices that can be eaten or crafted into seeds.

Basic plants

The preceding section deals with the classic crops, which provide a moderate farming experience. The next several sections describe other "growing things" that can be exploited.

Sugar cane

Sugar cane consists of green reeds that grow naturally near bodies of water, and collecting at least one sugar cane block is enough to start a farm, similar to the one shown in Figure 5-7. Sugar cane is useful to mass-produce: Paper and items such as bookcases require a lot of reeds to craft, and you can make sugar for items such as cake and potions of swiftness.

Figure 5-7: Growing reeds and cacti

Fortunately, sugar cane is easy to farm. Simply follow these steps:

1. **Find (or make) a place that holds water.**

   Reeds grow only near lakes or pools. Note that they can grow only on grass, dirt, or sand.

2. **Place canes next to the water in the same way you would place any block.**

When a patch of reeds is placed where it can grow, it extends vertically until it's three blocks tall.

3. **After the sugar cane is fully grown, harvest all but the bottom block.**

When you break the stalk blocks in the middle, the top section breaks down into items. The reeds at the bottom begin growing again.

The essential concept here is to plant a short patch of reeds, let it grow, and then mow it down so that it can grow again.

When the ground is flat, you're at eye level with the point at which you should break your sugar canes. Walk around with the crosshair at eye level, while holding the left mouse button to break all the reeds quickly.

Cacti

Cacti are sharp desert plants that can be used for creating traps or making green dye. (Refer to the small cactus farm shown in Figure 5-7.) You can typically find cacti in the desert, and you can grow them similarly to sugar cane (as described in the preceding section). However, growing them is unique because they

✔ Require no water and must be placed on sand

✔ Cannot be placed next to other blocks

✔ Are sharp, and they destroy items

Destroy the entire cactus and replant it to ensure that some of your profits aren't destroyed by other cactus blocks.

Cocoa beans

Cocoa beans are used to make brown dye and as an ingredient in cookies. The best way to find cocoa beans is to explore a jungle — the beans are found in pods growing off the trees. Though green and yellow pods aren't fully matured, orange ones provide several cocoa beans when you smash them.

Farming cocoa beans is easy. To place a pod, right-click some jungle wood while holding cocoa beans. Then break the pod when it turns orange to harvest lots of cocoa beans. Make a large wall of jungle wood to start your farm.

Nether wart

You can find *nether wart* growing in special rooms in the nether fortress (described in Chapter 8). You can pick up nether wart by breaking fully grown crops, as shown in Figure 5-8. Nether wart is useful for brewing potions (described in Chapter 6). You can farm nether wart by planting it in soul sand blocks and waiting for it to grow, similarly to wheat. (You don't need to till soul sand.)

Figure 5-8: Growing nether wart

Trees

Tree farms aren't commonly established. They're usually useful when you live in a place with few trees nearby or when you want a wood source while underground. To grow trees, collect saplings — occasionally dropped when breaking leaf blocks — and then right-click to place them on dirt or grass in a well-lit area. (Remember that trees need lots of space to grow.)

If you plant a square of four jungle saplings and apply bone meal to one of them, a giant tree grows.

Animals

You can use animal farms to acquire resources such as pork or wool without having to endure a lot of hassle. Animals follow you while you're holding wheat, so lure some into a fenced-in area to start your farm. Chickens are lured by seeds instead.

Right-clicking two animals of the same species while holding wheat (use seeds for chickens) causes them to spawn a baby animal. Thus, you can make use of your animal farm however you want and keep it populated.

A lamb's wool will be the same color as its parents' wool. To farm a specific color of wool, right-click some sheep while holding dye to paint them, and then start a farm with them. Sheep regrow shorn wool by eating grass.

Mushrooms

Though mushrooms slowly spread if their climate is dark enough, the spacious dark areas of a farm can attract monsters. If you don't want to have to perfect the lighting, use bone meal on a planted mushroom so that it grows into a giant mushroom, as shown in Figure 5-9. Giant mushrooms provide a huge profit when you break them and can be used to quickly get lots of mushrooms.

Figure 5-9: Giant mushrooms

6

Surviving through Invention

In This Chapter

▷ Advancing your architecture to the next level

▷ Building circuits with redstone

▷ Enchanting weapons, tools, and armor with special powers

▷ Playing in Creative mode

*T*his advanced chapter guides you through the more technical, inventive aspects of Minecraft. You find out how to build amazing structures, machines, and circuits, enchant tools with special powers, brew potions, and experiment with inventiveness in Creative mode. Even if it takes some time to master these concepts, it's worth the effort.

Building Masterpieces

Building is one of those satisfying hobbies in Minecraft that always instills a sense of accomplishment, though you can never truly finish. When you're ready to build a giant mansion, castle, tree fort, or another building, follow these steps to complete it quickly:

1. **Harvest the primary building materials.**

   Chop down trees, dig quarries, or collect coal and smelt smooth stone — collect in one sweep all the blocks you can so that you don't have to return later. To build a wooden structure, for example, keep in mind that almost all wooden blocks are made by throwing together planks and sticks; simply gather what you need — and a little more. See whether you can accomplish other goals during this phase as well. You may need several hundred blocks for major projects.

2. **Go to the crafting table and use a portion of the raw materials to make stairs, slabs, ladders, fences, and gates (as described in Chapter 4).**

   Always craft more than you think you'll need, to ensure that you don't have to return to the crafting table. Alternatively, take the crafting table with you.

3. **Build the frame of the structure and fill it.**

   You can build the structure however you want from here. For detail, try adding items such as stairs, slabs, and trapdoors. (Figure 6-1 shows you an example.) You can also place slabs and stair blocks on ceilings to make upside-down moldings. Stairs and slabs are useful because they can be made from several different materials.

Figure 6-1: Detailed arrangement

Engineering with Redstone

Redstone is one of the more advanced concepts in Minecraft. You can obtain *redstone* dust by mining redstone ore underground. You can spread this dust across the ground as wire, attach it to levers or doors, and craft it into torches and repeaters to build machines. Whether you want a lever that performs two tasks at a time, a combination lock, or a giant virtual computer, you can build it by cleverly arranging redstone dust.

If you read this section from start to finish, start a new game in Creative mode (see the section "Playing in Creative mode," later in this chapter) and follow along by building machines yourself. If you're new to Minecraft, this chapter is somewhat advanced. Use the later section "Applying redstone circuits" as a technical reference guide.

Transmitting power with redstone wire

Put simply, redstone dust carries power. While holding a lump of redstone dust, right-click the ground to place it there, at which point it becomes a *redstone wire*. In its default state, the redstone wire is uncharged, which means that it does nothing.

When the redstone is powered by a device such as a lever, tripwire, button, or pressure plate, the wire begins to glow red and transmits power to open doors, ignite explosives, or activate dispensers. Figure 6-2 shows a pressure plate connected to a mechanism that ignites three explosives at a time.

Figure 6-2: Basic mechanism

Redstone dust can transmit power and perform more tasks than you can normally complete by pulling a lever. You should know these concepts about redstone dust. It can:

- **Orient itself automatically:** When you first place some redstone dust, it appears as a small lump of wire that can transmit power in all directions. By placing more dust or certain mechanisms near it, the wire stretches into lines, corners, and bends to meet its task.

- **Extend 15 blocks from the power source:** Charged redstone wire gets dimmer as it moves away from its power source. After the wire travels 15 blocks from any power source, it can no longer transmit energy that far. Use mechanisms or items such as redstone repeaters (described in the next section) to extend it farther.

- **Climb blocks:** Your designs don't just have to be two-dimensional. Redstone wire can run up or down the side of a single block so that you can build staircases to carry the circuit vertically. However, the redstone still has to have an unbroken path, as shown in Figure 6-3.

By carrying power in your world, you can achieve great accomplishments by simply pressing a button.

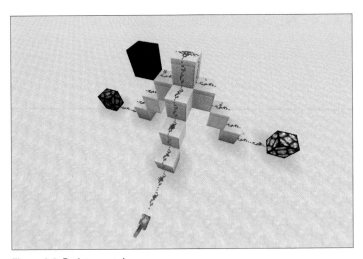

Figure 6-3: Redstone staircase

Using other redstone mechanisms

Of course, you can craft other items to improve your redstone creations. These allow you to build advanced circuits and accomplish more interesting goals.

Although a block such as grass or iron technically absorbs no current, I sometimes refer to it as *powered*. See the later section "Applying redstone circuits" for rules governing powered blocks.

Redstone torch

A *redstone torch* is a useful resource that's crafted with redstone dust and a stick. It provides a constant source of power to everything next to it, above it, and below it, and it can be placed on floors or walls. It can even power the block directly above it.

Redstone torches never burn out on their own, but you can turn them off by powering the blocks they're placed on, as shown in Figure 6-4.

Redstone torches are important because they're power sources that can be turned off by other parts of the circuit. Thus, the clever arrangement of redstone torches can allow for powerful circuits such as combination locks or programs.

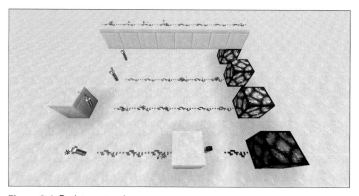

Figure 6-4: Redstone torches

Redstone repeater

Redstone repeaters are interesting little mechanisms that can be placed on the ground like redstone wire, though they have a few extra faculties. They

- **Transmit current in only one direction:** When you place a repeater, the output faces away from you. Repeaters also transmit current after a brief delay.

- **Allow you to add a delay to the circuit:** Right-click a repeater to edit the time it takes for the current to pass. Use a delay to make timers and choreograph large circuits.

- **Extend a wire's 15-block range:** Then the circuits can move as far as you want.

Figure 6-5 shows examples of using redstone repeaters.

Figure 6-5: Redstone repeaters

In addition, if you place a redstone repeater so that it powers a second one from the side, it locks the second repeater's On–Off value. Then the circuit can store binary memory, which is useful in advanced designs.

Run a redstone repeater into a block to easily make a powered block.

Applying redstone circuits

Of course, you can accomplish a great deal by using circuits. Open doors, move blocks with pistons, ignite explosives, play music, or complete basic tasks, for example. The following list describes additional redstone-based items and their uses, as well as mechanical items that can be powered by redstone:

- ✔ **Redstone wire:** A wire that powers adjacent wires and repeaters, the block it rests on, and any block or mechanism it faces. For more information, see "Transmitting power with redstone wire," earlier in this chapter.

- ✔ **Powered blocks:** Technical terminology used in this chapter. Ice and glass cannot be powered. These blocks power all adjacent mechanisms.

- ✔ **Redstone torch:** A power source that affects every adjacent mechanism, including ones above and below; it also powers the block just above it. I discuss redstone torches in more detail in the earlier section "Redstone torch."

- ✔ **Redstone repeater:** A block that's powered by anything behind it and powers anything in front of it with a slight delay. See the earlier section "Redstone repeater."

- ✔ **Lever:** A type of switch that affects adjacent mechanisms as well as the block it's placed on. You can turn a lever on or off by right-clicking it. You can place a lever on any surface.

- ✔ **Button:** A type of switch that sends a temporary current to adjacent mechanisms as well as to the block it's placed on. In addition to right-clicking it, you can activate a wooden button by shooting it with an arrow. You can place buttons only on walls.

- ✔ **Tripwire hook:** A type of switch that affects adjacent mechanisms as well as the block it's placed on. Tripwire hooks can be placed only on walls. Place string in a line between two hooks to make *tripwire* — the hooks are powered when the tripwire is stepped on or when the string is broken without shears.

- ✔ **Pressure plate:** A type of switch that transmits power to adjacent mechanisms and to the block it's placed on, when weighted down. Wood pressure plates can be activated by any entity, whereas stone pressure plates can be activated only by an entity that is at least as large as a chicken.

- ✔ **Detector rail:** A type of rail that works similarly to a pressure plate. It transmits power when a minecart crosses over it, and it affects adjacent mechanisms and the block it's placed on.

✒ **Redstone lamp:** A lamp that emits light as long as it's powered. It is also a full block, so it can share the properties of a powered block.

✒ **Booster rail:** A charged minecart track that powers other booster rails (within a 9-block range). When powered, the booster rail speeds up minecarts; when it isn't powered, it slows them to a halt.

✒ **Piston:** A device that pushes blocks but destroys redstone devices. Pushing blocks can affect circuits. A piston can be activated by any power source.

✒ **Doors, fence gates, trapdoors, TNT, dispensers, and note blocks:** Mechanical items that can be activated by any power source (as described in the appendix, at `www.dummies.com/go/minecraftfd`).

Advanced redstone circuitry

You can do lots of fun things with redstone, even such tasks as building computers, calculators, and virtual RAM. First, you need to understand how to build redstone circuitry.

The NOT gate

Suppose that a redstone wire passes through your circuit. If you run the wire through a NOT gate, the wire reverses its value: Off becomes On, and On becomes Off. This is useful for commands such as, "If the pressure plate isn't being triggered, play the All Clear music." The NOT gate, shown in Figure 6-6, is based on torches being naturally active, though they can be turned off by active current.

The OR gate

Arguably one of the simplest gates, the OR gate says, "If either of these redstone currents is activated, turn on this third current." To make one of these gates, you simply connect two separate circuits.

NOT gate   OR gate   AND gate   XOR gate

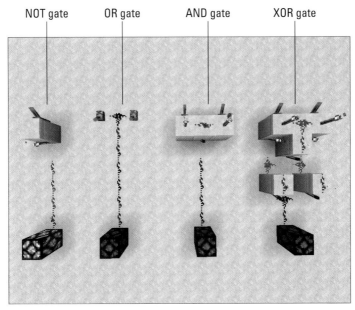

Figure 6-6: Building NOT, OR, AND, and XOR gates

The AND gate

The AND gate is tricky to set up. How do you say, "Turn on this circuit only if both of these two other circuits are running?" The setup shown in Figure 6-6 is one of the easiest, though the concepts behind it are useful to understand.

The XOR gate

The XOR gate means, "Turn on this circuit if only one of these other two circuits is running." The solution shown in Figure 6-6 may be somewhat complicated, but it's simply AND, NOT, and OR rolled into one: The OR gate turns on the output if either lever is activated, and the AND and NOT gates turn it off again if both levers are down.

Multicircuitous designs

To continue your experience in redstone engineering, replace the levers in the basic gates with redstone wire and hook the gates together. Figure 6-7 shows two different ways to build an advanced circuit, with a diagram of the circuit for comparison, as shown in Figure 6-8.

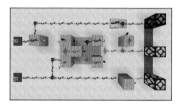

Figure 6-7: Advanced redstone design

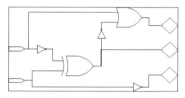

Figure 6-8: Circuit diagram

 In case you're interested, this circuit adds 3 to any 2-digit binary input, expressing the answer in binary form.

 If you don't fully understand the concepts explained in this section but you still want to use redstone, simply copy the models I provide or study other people's designs on the Internet. Hide your mechanisms underground if you want them to function without being out in the open.

Enchanting Weapons, Tools, and Armor

Enchanting is a tool that's helpful to use after you have spent some time in Minecraft and gathered a lot of materials. Using this process, you imbue certain items with special powers that make them more effective — for example, you can make a pickaxe mine faster or make a pair of boots that mitigates damage inflicted by falling.

Enchantment tables, which are used to enchant items, are crafted from diamond, obsidian, and a book. (For the recipe, see the appendix, which is available for download at www. dummies.com/go/minecraftfd). You generally need only one of these tables, which you place on the ground to begin enchanting. Don't worry about losing your diamonds; enchantment tables are much too durable to be destroyed by creepers or other hazards.

Enchanting an item

After you create an enchantment table, follow these steps to enchant an item:

1. **Right-click the enchantment table to open the Enchanting menu.**

   The Enchanting menu, shown in Figure 6-9, consists of a square (where you can place the tool, weapon, or armor to enchant) and three tablet slots that show available enchantments.

Figure 6-9: Enchanting menu

2. **Place in the square the item you want to enchant.**

   If the item can be enchanted, three tablets appear, each showing a green number (with the largest in the bottom row). This is the level of the enchantment — the green number above the Experience bar represents the number of levels you have to spend on enchantments. Tablets appear grayed-out when you don't have the necessary points to use them.

3. **Click an available tablet to ascribe the selected item with a random enchantment.**

   The higher the number is on the tablet, the higher the chance of getting a powerful enchantment!

Powering up

Tablets can reach Level 30 to provide especially strong enchantments. Unfortunately, if the enchantment table is placed without bookshelves, you can't surpass Level 8. If you have a lot of experience orbs and want the best of the best, you have to power up the enchantment table.

To improve the enchantment table, you have to place bookshelves nearby. When a bookshelf is near an enchantment table, the table absorbs information from it and produces higher-level tablets. However, bookshelves have to be arranged in a certain way: As many as 32 of them can be placed around a single enchantment table, as shown in Figure 6-10.

Figure 6-10: Powerful enchantment table

Only 15 of these bookshelves are required in order to access a Level 30 tablet, and you can subtract more if you lack experience orbs. However, to get 15 bookshelves, you have to harvest 135 sugar canes and kill approximately 45 cows. Ascribing low-level enchantments to some items while you get more bookshelves can be worthwhile.

Using enchantments

When an item is enchanted, it shows the names of all of its enchantments under the item label. Some enchantments are followed by Roman numerals (such as I, II, III, IV, and V), representing the level of that particular enchantment. Enchantments are passive and take effect when you use the enchanted item. Available enchantments are detailed in Tables 6-1 through 6-4.

Table 6-1 Enchantments: Pickaxe, Axe, Shovel

Enchantment	Possible Levels	Effect
Efficiency	I, II, III, IV, V	The tool breaks blocks much faster than a normal tool.
Unbreaking	I, II, III	The tool is more durable and can break more blocks before it shatters.
Fortune	I, II, III	Any block that cannot be replaced when broken, such as diamond ore and melon blocks, has a chance of giving extra loot. Gravel has a higher chance of providing flint when broken.
Silk touch	I	This special enchantment allows you to obtain any block you break as an item, even if it would normally drop another item, such as coal ore and stone. A silk touch item cannot be enchanted with fortune at the same time, and it cannot harvest certain blocks such as monster spawners.

Table 6-2	Enchantments: Sword	
Enchantment	*Possible Levels*	*Effect*
Sharpness, smite, bane of arthropods	I, II, III, IV, V	These enchantments boost the sword's damage and cannot be active at the same time. Smite deals extra damage to the undead, and the bane of arthropods deals extra damage to bugs. Sharpness inflicts slightly less extra damage.
Knockback	I, II	Attacking an entity with this enchantment knocks it backward much farther than with a normal attack.
Looting	I, II, III	Enemies you slay with this sword can drop more items and have a higher chance of rewarding you with rare items.
Fire aspect	I, II	Enemies you hit with this sword are lit on fire and take constant damage over time.

Table 6-3	Enchantments: Armor	
Enchantment	*Possible Levels*	*Effect*
(Fire/blast/projectile) protection	I, II, III, IV	Only one protection enchantment at a time can be used, and it increases the defensive capacity of the armor. There are four types of this enchantment that can guard you against burning, explosions, or ranged weapons — the classic "protection" enchantment protects against all damage.
Respiration (helmet only)	I, II, III	You can hold your breath underwater much longer while wearing this helmet.

Enchantment	Possible Levels	Effect
Aqua affinity (helmet only)	I	Normally, you break blocks much slower while underwater. You can mitigate this effect by wearing this helmet.
Feather falling (boots only)	I, II, III, IV	These boots let you take less damage from falling.

Table 6-4   Enchantments: Bow

Enchantment	Possible Levels	Effect
Power	I, II, III, IV	Arrows fired by this bow inflict bonus damage.
Punch	I, II	This bow is extra strong, knocking its targets backward.
Flame	I	Arrows fired by this bow are ignited and can set targets on fire, inflicting damage over time.
Infinity	I	This bow doesn't consume ammunition, so you can use it as long as you have at least one arrow. You can't retrieve arrows fired by this bow.

Some powerful enchantments have several of these effects. For example, you might obtain a pickaxe with Efficiency IV, Unbreaking II, and Fortune I. You can combine enchanted items with an anvil if you didn't get the enchantment you want and you want to improve it — this process is described in the bonus chapter, available for download at www.dummies.com/ go/minecraftfd.

Brewing Potions

Brewing potions is another faculty available to you as you progress in Minecraft. After you obtain a blaze rod, a fairly high-end item, you can craft it with cobblestone to make a *brewing stand*, as described in the appendix, available for download at www.dummies.com/go/minecraftfd. This item is used to mix and set potions, which you can drink or throw to cause various effects.

To obtain a considerable number of potions, you need a good supply of glass blocks and nether wart. You can craft glass by smelting sand in a furnace, and you can find nether wart in nether fortresses and farm it, as explained in Chapter 5.

Build your brewing stand near your nether wart farm, to get all you need while you need it.

Brewing basic potions

At the time of this writing, you can brew 11 kinds of potions, each with one or two modifications and a *splash* version that can be thrown. To brew potions, follow these steps (and see Figure 6-11):

1. **Craft glass into bottles (as described in Chapter 4) and then right-click a water source or a cauldron to fill them with water.**

   These bottles can be brewed into potions. Craft enough bottles to make all the potions you want.

2. **Right-click the brewing stand and place some water bottles in the slots.**

   Use three bottles for maximum efficiency.

3. **Add the base ingredient.**

   You usually add nether wart as the base ingredient, but you can add a fermented spider eye if you want to make only a potion of weakness (described later in this section).

4. **Add the secondary ingredients.**

   If you used nether wart, the water bottles turn into awkward potions, which have no effect. However, you can keep these potions on the brewing stand and add more ingredients to give them the characteristics you need; see Table 6-5.

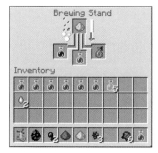

Figure 6-11: Brewing menu

Table 6-5		Basic Potions
Ingredient	*Potion*	*Effect*
Glistering melon	Potion of healing	Some health is restored.
Blaze powder	Potion of strength	You inflict more damage under this effect.
Ghast tear	Potion of regeneration	Your health rapidly regenerates.
Sugar	Potion of swiftness	You can run much faster.
Magma cream	Potion of fire resistance	You take much less damage from fire. This potion is a good one to use while fighting Blaze.
Golden carrot	Potion of night vision	You can see much better in the dark.
Spider eye	Potion of poison	Damage is dealt to you over time; useless for now.
Fermented spider eye	Potion of weakness	Your attack power is reduced temporarily; useless for now.

Using potions

To use a potion, select the potion and hold down the right mouse button to drink it. Though potions of healing have an instantaneous effect, others can last for a couple of minutes.

Any potion effects that you might have are shown when you open the inventory screen.

If you're afflicted with an effect such as wither or weakness, which can be dangerous, drink a bucket of milk to cleanse all potion effects. You can obtain milk by selecting a bucket and right-clicking a cow.

Modifying potions

After you brew some potions, you may want to modify their effects. You can brew four different ingredients into the potions to modify them:

- **Redstone dust:** Increases the duration of a non-instantaneous potion, allowing you to retain its effects for a long time. It cancels out the effects of glowstone, described in the next bullet.

- **Glowstone dust:** Makes potions stronger and more effective, if possible. It cancels out the effects of redstone.

- **Gunpowder:** Turns potions into *splash potions*, which have a differently shaped bottle, and you can throw these potions by right-clicking. When a splash potion hits an object, it explodes, applying the potion's effect to everything nearby. If you have a harmful potion such as Poison, turn it into a splash potion and throw it at your enemies! Unfortunately, throwing a splash potion destroys the bottle. See the "Brewing splash potions" section, later in this chapter, for more information.

- **Fermented spider eye:** Used on a potion with a positive effect, reverses the effect, as explained in the next section.

Brewing negative potions

In addition to the helpful potions described earlier in this chapter, Minecraft has a whole class of negative potions, which generally have a negative effect. You can make and use negative potions by adding a fermented spider eye to potions, as described in Table 6-6.

Table 6-6	Brewing Negative Potions	
Negative Potion	**Reagent**	**Effect**
Potion of slowness	Potion of swiftness or fire resistance	You walk much slower.
Potion of harming	Potion of healing or poison	This potion instantly deals damage.
Potion of weakness	Potion of strength or regeneration	This potion reduces your attack power. However, you can brew it by simply adding a fermented spider eye to a water bottle.
Potion of invisibility	Potion of night vision	You become invisible, and you cannot be seen by anything unless you're wearing armor.

As with other potions, you can modify these potions with red-stone, glowstone, or gunpowder.

Brewing splash potions

Of course, some potions seem fairly useless because their effect on you is negative. When you use a splash potion, you can instantly apply potions to anything you want. Simply brew gunpowder into any potion and it becomes a powerful projectile that you can throw by selecting it and right-clicking.

Splash potions are useful for a number of reasons, including these:

- ✔ If you craft splash potions of healing, you can throw them on the ground to instantly heal yourself (and everything around you).
- ✔ You can throw splash potions of slowness into a group of enemies to make a quick escape or use potions of harming to bring them down.

All undead, such as zombies and skeletons, are immune to poison, and potions of harming only heal them. If an undead is nearby, use a splash potion of healing to hurt the undead and heal yourself.

Witches and potions

You can clearly see the effects of potions when you fight witches. These enemies, who are difficult to beat, live in huts in the swamp. When they take damage, they drink potions of regeneration, and they use potions of fire resistance to avoid burning. They also throw an assortment of splash potions at you to weaken, poison, slow, and damage you. However, if you defeat a witch, she drops an assortment of potion reagents, including the occasional nether wart. Witches are detailed in Chapter 7.

Creatively Improving Your World

This short section orients you to some inventive tasks you can undertake to improve your Minecraft home. Of course, you can either figure out how to use specific inventions or simply work to the best of your ability. Using basic items such as water buckets and pistons, you can perform tasks such as these:

- **Farm wheat quickly.** You can use dispensers or pistons to send water rushing over crops, uprooting them, and letting the loot drift into a little output area.

- **Farm cacti automatically.** Cacti cannot be placed next to another block, so let them grow into such a position. They fall apart, and the item blocks can be channeled through a canal to provide a constant source of cactus blocks.

- **Farm monsters.** By building a dark room or exploiting a dungeon (see Chapter 8), you can use water canals to push monsters into a certain area and collect their loot easily.

- **Build advanced transportation.** Use minecart rails to cut travel time and mitigate hunger. You can also use pistons to build ornate doors and secret passageways.

- **Build defenses.** Utilities such as dispensers can be used to bring down any enemy hiding outside your door. Fill a dispenser with arrows or harmful potions, and connect it to a lever inside your house.

✓ **Create adventures.** In Chapter 10, I discuss Adventure mode and the process of building and downloading adventure worlds. You can use redstone devices and other mechanisms to build challenges for other players to try.

Playing in Creative Mode

Most of this book focuses on the various faculties of Survival mode, so this section covers the simpler, but still notable, part of the game: Creative mode.

You enter Creative mode by creating a new world and clicking the Game Mode button to change the game type. Alternatively, in a world where cheats are available, you can enter Creative mode by using this command:

```
/gamemode 1
```

You can return to Survival mode by using this command:

```
/gamemode 0
```

In Creative mode, you can build whatever you want with no fear of restraint or resource consumption. You can use this mode whenever you're feeling creative rather than adventurous and you want to try new ideas. In Creative mode, you can

✓ **Place blocks while retaining inventory:** If you use a consumable item in Creative mode, it takes effect, but the item isn't consumed.

✓ **Break blocks instantly:** Clicking blocks always breaks them immediately, regardless of the tool you use.

✓ **Press the spacebar while airborne to fly:** While flying, use the spacebar to go up and the Shift key to go down. You can stop flying by touching the ground or double-tapping the spacebar.

✓ **Avoid all damage:** You have no health or hunger, and nothing can kill you. The only way to die is to dig through the bedrock at the bottom of the world and fall deep into the Void, which is difficult to do accidentally.

✔ **Use items without consuming durability or ammunition:** Tools, weapons, and armor don't lose durability when used, and you can fire a bow without consuming arrows. You can also perform any enchantment without the necessary experience orbs.

✔ **Add any item you want to your inventory:** Rather than see the standard inventory screen, you pick and choose the items you want in the Creative mode inventory. The inventory consists of 12 tabs. The 10 on the left are categories of items, the Compass tab lets you search for items by name, and the Chest tab shows your Survival-style inventory, as shown in Figure 6-12.

Figure 6-12: Creative mode inventory

7

Understanding the Natural World

In This Chapter

▷ Recognizing different biomes

▷ Studying docile, hostile, and neutral mobs

▷ Obtaining resources from biomes and mobs

*I*n addition to gathering, fighting, and building, exploring is a fun and useful component of Minecraft. You can explore mountains, deserts, tundra, and jungles to obtain the resources you need. This chapter describes the features and appeals of various biomes and gives you an overview of the creatures you'll face along the way.

Sightseeing in the Biomes

A *biome* is a specific climate that defines the look and feel of an area in the world. Biomes, which never change, are strictly defined by their looks and faculties. You encounter many different types of biomes in Minecraft, as shown in Figure 7-1.

Figure 7-1: Intersecting biomes

Biomes and their features are described in this list:

- **Desert:** This arid biome is full of dead shrubs and cacti, and the ground is sand, with a layer of sandstone underneath. The desert is the home to many structures detailed in Chapter 8, such as villages, wells, and pyramids. Rain doesn't fall in the desert, even when it's pouring everywhere else.

  Features: Sand, sandstone, cacti, desert villages, desert wells, desert temples, no rain

- **End:** The End can be reached only by finding and entering an end portal (see Chapter 3). It's the only place where you can find end stone, and you can gain lots of experience orbs by slaying the ender dragon. Giant, obsidian pillars provide a reliable source of obsidian, and you can get a lot of ender pearls by fighting the endermen who wander around.

  Features: End stone, obsidian, endermen, ender dragon

- **Forest:** You can harvest a lot of trees from the forest, and it has grass for growing crops — though it can grow especially dark at night.

  Features: Oak and birch trees, grass, occasional wolves

✏ **Hills:** In addition to the hills that sometimes appear in other biomes, the Extreme Hills biome is full of giant, grassy obelisks and mountains. It's the only biome under which you can occasionally find emerald ore, and it's an excellent place to build mountainside hideouts.

Features: Grass, emerald

✏ **Ice plains:** This plain is covered in a layer of snow, and the surface of nearby water is frozen solid. You can't find many resources here, but you can scoop up the snow with a shovel to form snowballs and craft snow blocks. Rain turns to snow in this biome, replacing any snow that you may have shoveled.

Features: Snow, sparse oak trees

✏ **Jungle:** Though somewhat difficult to navigate, with lots of trees and undergrowth, jungles contain many unique resources. Jungle trees can be used to make reddish wood and grow cocoa beans, ocelots can be tamed as pet cats, and jungle temples can be explored to find lots of useful items, as described in Chapter 8.

Features: Jungle trees, cocoa plants, lakes, vines, ocelots, jungle temples

✏ **Mushroom Island:** This extremely rare biome, which appears next to oceans, is made of the purple grass *mycelium*, which can spread quickly onto dirt blocks. This biome is full of giant mushrooms, and the only naturally appearing creature is the *mooshroom,* a cow that resembles a red mushroom.

Features: Mycelium, giant mushrooms, mooshrooms

✏ **Nether:** This biome cannot be naturally found. It's accessible only via a nether portal, as described in Chapter 3. Although the Nether is dangerous, it's useful for several reasons: You can obtain netherrack, with its special ability to burn indefinitely; nether wart and the soul sand to farm it; nether bricks for building; and lots of lava. You can also kill monsters to gain useful items such as gold nuggets, ghast tears, wither skulls, magma cream, and blaze rods.

Features: Netherrack, soul sand, gravel, lava, nether monsters, nether fortresses

✔ **Ocean:** The ocean is a huge biome, with no easily visible use; however, the bottom of the ocean is rich in clay deposits. You can also explore the ocean in a boat to look for caves or ravines at the bottom.

Features: Water, clay

✔ **Plains:** This simple, flat grassland is useful for collecting items such as seeds and flowers, and it provides an open area for maneuvering. You can also see much farther from the plains because the flat ground helps you spot other biomes and features. You can occasionally find villages on the plains, as explained in Chapter 8.

Features: Grass, village

✔ **River:** The river is a winding canal that separates certain biomes. Some rivers run through snowy biomes and are completely frozen.

Features: Water, clay

✔ **Swamp:** This darkly colored biome is half land and half shallow water, with overgrown trees and large clay deposits at the bottom of its murky lakes. You can find slimes here (as detailed later in this chapter). You can also find witch huts built in the swamp, which house a powerful enemy.

Features: Oak trees, mushrooms, vines, lily pads, water, clay, slimes, witch huts

✔ **Taiga:** This snowy forest is perfect for finding wolves, which roam the forest and can be tamed. As on the ice plain, the taiga snows rather than rains.

Features: Snow, spruce trees, wolves

✔ **Underground:** Though the underground technically isn't a biome, its rich ecosystem is worth mentioning. The underground contains caverns full of ores and darkness, making it useful but dangerous. It can also house structures such as dungeons, mine shafts, strongholds, and ravines.

Features: Ores, caverns, abandoned mine shafts, Strongholds, dungeons, ravines, stone

If you ever need a resource that you can't find nearby, explore and look for a biome that offers it.

Examining Different Types of Mobs

A *mob* refers to any creature, monster, or other living entity that you may find in the world. At the time of this writing, Minecraft has 30 different mobs, each with different faculties that drop various loot when slain, including experience orbs.

Docile mobs

Some mobs in Minecraft are *docile:* They can't harm you, and they won't try. All land-based docile mobs (such as pigs, cows, sheep, chickens, ocelots, villagers, and mooshrooms) flee when attacked. You can also lure pigs, cows, and sheep around by holding wheat, and you can right-click two animals of the same species while holding wheat, to feed them and cause them to spawn a baby animal. Chickens have this same faculty, but they require seeds instead of wheat.

This list describes the types of docile mobs, many of which are shown in Figure 7-2:

✔ A member of a flying mob, the **bat** adds atmospheric visuals to dark caverns. In addition to flying, it sleeps on the underside of blocks.

✔ The **chicken,** which is easier than other creatures to kill, is a good source of feathers. It can be bred (with seeds instead of wheat), and it occasionally lays eggs, which can be picked up. It incurs no damage from falling.

✔ The common **cow** provides useful loot, and it can be bred. To get a bucket of milk, right-click a cow while holding an empty bucket.

✔ A **mooshroom** is a red cow that appears on the Mushroom Islands. It can be bred, and you can shear it to get red mushrooms and turn it into a standard cow. Right-click a mooshroom while holding a bowl to create mushroom stew.

✔ The timid jungle cat known as an **ocelot** can be tamed and domesticated. Living only in the jungle, it's frightened by an avatar's movement. If it tentatively approaches you while you're holding raw fish, right-click to feed it. You can feed an ocelot five times or so to tame it.

 ✔ A commonly occurring animal and a good food source, the **pig** can be bred, and it turns into a zombie pigman when struck by lightning.

 ✔ The common **sheep** can be used to obtain wool instead of food. Its wool comes in several different colors. It can be bred; right-click a sheep while holding shears to obtain 1 to 3 blocks of wool; right-click a sheep while holding dye to recolor the sheep. Baby sheep have the same color as their parents; sheep eat grass to regrow wool.

 ✔ The water-dwelling **squid** is a source of black dye. It can swim, and it will die if it has no water to breathe.

 ✔ The **villager** lives in a village and trades items with you, as described in Chapter 8. Villagers remain indoors at night, and they can fall in love and have children. They can also trade with players.

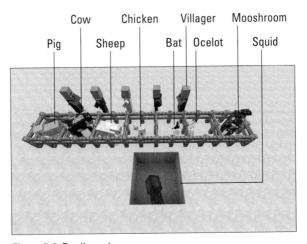

Cow   Chicken   Villager   Mooshroom

Pig   Sheep   Bat   Ocelot   Squid

Figure 7-2: Docile mobs

Hostile mobs

Hostile mobs, as shown in Figure 7-3, cause most of the danger in Minecraft: They attack you without provocation. However, hostile mobs tend to provide especially useful loot.

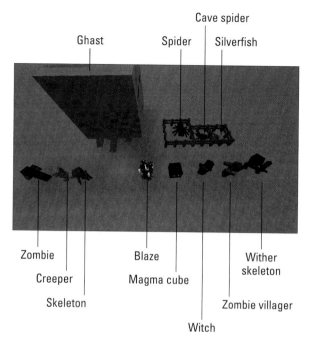

Ghast   Spider   Cave spider   Silverfish

Zombie   Creeper   Skeleton   Blaze   Magma cube   Witch   Wither skeleton   Zombie villager

Figure 7-3: Hostile mobs

This list describes hostile mobs in detail:

✓ A powerful guardian of the nether fortresses, the **Blaze** is a fiery construct that provides a useful item. It can fly, it shoots fireballs, and it takes damage from snowballs.

✓ The poisonous **cave spider** lurks around abandoned mine shafts. An *arthropod,* it's fast, climbs walls, and jumps. It poisons targets in Normal mode or Hardcore mode.

✓ The plant-like enemy known as the **creeper** walks up to you and explodes. It's destructive, and it deals massive damage by exploding, though it cannot use melee attacks. It becomes incredibly powerful when struck by lightning.

✓ The **ender dragon** is a giant dragon that is the final battle of the game. It's an enemy that appears in the End, flying around and occasionally charging for massive damage. See Chapter 3 for details and tactics.

✏ The giant, floating beast of the Nether, the **ghast** spits fireballs that can be hit back at it. It can fly, and it's destructive, hard to hit, and not resilient.

 ✏ A **magma cube** is the slime of the Nether — it bounces like a spring. It splits into smaller cubes when killed. Larger cubes are more armored.

 ✏ A **silverfish** is a nipping bug that burrows into stone. An *arthropod*, it can hide inside stone, cobblestone, and stone bricks. Active silverfish can awaken hidden silverfish to rally a swarm.

 ✏ A **skeleton** is a powerful, skilled archer that drives off foes with its arrows. It's an *undead,* and some skeletons can equip armor or weapons.

 ✏ A bouncing blob of **slime** appears in various sizes in swamps and, occasionally, in deep caves. It splits into smaller slimes when killed: Tiny slimes are harmless and can be kept as pets.

 ✏ The **spider,** a quick enemy, is difficult to outrun and escape. An *arthropod*, it becomes neutral in daylight and doesn't attack unless provoked. It's fast, wall-climbing, and jumping.

 ✏ A **witch** is a master alchemist who lives in a hut in the swamp and attacks with an assortment of potions. She drinks potions of regeneration to heal and uses potions to mitigate fire damage. She throws potions of weakness, poison, slowness, and harming.

 ✏ A **wither skeleton** is a powerful warrior that patrols nether fortresses. It's an undead, it inflicts high damage, and it's immune to fire. (Some wither skeletons can equip weapons and armor.) It inflicts wither damage to the player in Normal or Hardcore difficulty mode, draining the Health bar temporarily and potentially causing death.

 ✏ The **wither** is a flying undead construct that is a powerful foe. It's a destructive, unique undead. You can create the wither with four blocks of soul sand and three wither skeleton skulls. (Refer to the "Constructs" section of the bonus chapter, available for download at www.dummies.com/go/minecraftfd.) Stay away from the wither as it comes to life, because it creates a sizable explosion. The wither flies around and throws exploding skulls at everything it sees, and it can smash its way through blocks. It also regenerates over time, and it drains health from its victims to heal itself. After the wither loses half its health, it becomes immune to arrows. It drops a nether star.

 ✔ A **zombie** is a slow, lumbering enemy that inflicts damage on contact, and it appears commonly at night. An *undead* mob, it burns in daylight and slightly resists damage. Some zombies can equip items and wear armor.

 ✔ A **zombified villager** can appear naturally or whenever a villager is killed by a zombie in Normal mode or Hardcore mode. It has the same faculties as a zombie.

Neutral and allied mobs

Some mobs are *neutral*, leaving you alone until you provoke them. Minecraft has only a few neutral mobs, and some of them can become *allied* and fight alongside you, as described in this list and shown in Figure 7-4:

 ✔ A **cat,** which is a tamed ocelot, can follow you around. It attacks chickens and scares creepers. Right-click a cat to have it sit or follow you. It can be bred like certain passive mobs. (Use raw fish instead of wheat.)

 ✔ The **enderman** is a mysterious and rare nightfolk that originates from the End. Powerful and tall, it teleports for locomotion and to avoid damage; it dodges projectiles and detests water and sunlight. The enderman is provoked whenever you place the crosshair over it.

 ✔ The **iron golem** is a slow but powerful village guardian that is built by placing a pumpkin on top of a cross of iron blocks. (See the bonus chapter, available for download at www.dummies.com/go/minecraftfd.) Giant but slow, it attacks nearby hostile mobs or any player who attacks a villager. It flings targets into the air and inflicts massive damage, and it spawns naturally in some villages (see Chapter 8) or when built by the player.

 ✔ A **snow golem** can be built by putting a pumpkin on top of two snow blocks. This guardian trails snow as it walks, and it lobs snowballs at hostile mobs, knocking them back. Though harmed by water, with enough numbers it can kill Blaze. It explodes into snowballs when killed.

✔ The **wolf** is a wild dog that can be tamed. Don't attack it or else its entire group will charge you. While holding bones, right-click an unprovoked wolf a few times to feed it until it's tame; right-click tamed wolves while holding meat to feed and heal them. Right-clicking tamed wolves also tells them to sit or follow. Following wolves appear next to you if they can't reach you; tamed wolves attack your enemies but avoid creepers.

✔ The **zombie pigman** is a wanderer from the Nether that attacks you if you attack one of its brethren. Undead, it attacks in a swarm and wields a golden sword. Some zombie pigmen can equip better weapons and armor.

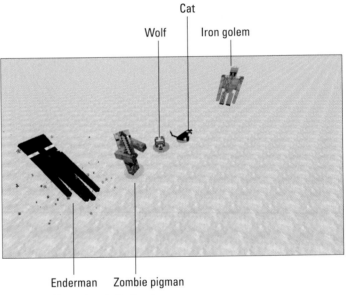

Figure 7-4: Neutral and allied mobs

8

Understanding the Man-Made World

*T*he amazing game Minecraft produces natural landscapes that look different every time you play. However, Minecraft is played not only in forests and on mountains but also — if you get lucky while exploring — in useful structures such as bustling villages, treasure-filled pyramids, or dangerous dungeons. This chapter helps you find and benefit from these structures to enhance your experience.

Trading in Villages

A *village* is a group of structures — such as hovels, smithies, churches and roads — arranged as a community for its residents, as shown in Figure 8-1. A village can appear as a plain or a desert (with a different motif for each one), and its inhabitants can prove helpful to you.

Exploring village features

Villages are composed of several different structures, each of which can be useful. Some of the components of a village are described in Table 8-1.

Figure 8-1: Village

Table 8-1   Village Features

Structure	Description	How to Use It
Hut, hovel, or house	A place of overnight shelter for villagers	Homes appear naturally, but you can build your own housing for villagers. (See the later section "Building a village.")
Farm	A flat stretch of farmland on which villagers grow crops	Help farm these crops to grow wheat, carrots, and potatoes.
Smithy	A cobblestone building that holds a forge and a storage chest with useful treasure; one or two may appear in a village	Look for these valuable items in the chest in the back room. You can also borrow the lava.
Well	A small structure that appears in a village and holds water	Use it as a reliable source of water; it's renewable.
Other buildings	Structures such as butcher shops, libraries, and churches	House villagers with specialized trading options (as explained in the later section "Trading with emeralds").

Villages that appear in deserts provide a source of smooth sandstone blocks. Replace broken blocks so that villagers' homes are safe during the night.

Trading with emeralds

To trade with a villager, right-click him and use emeralds as currency to buy and sell materials.

Though the most common villager is the farmer (wearing a brown robe), you have other trading options from butchers (white aprons), blacksmiths (black aprons), librarians (white robes), and priests (purple robes). Blacksmiths can be especially useful because they sometimes offer iron or diamond items, but at a steeper cost.

To trade with villagers, follow these steps:

1. **Right-click a villager to open the Trade menu, as shown in Figure 8-2.**

   The top of the Trade menu shows a large, gray arrow with an item to the right and one or two items to the left. The items to the left of the arrow are the ones the villager wants. If the villager wants to buy materials such as raw meat or paper, find some. If he wants to sell you items for emeralds, obtain some by selling to other villagers.

2. **Place the items that the villager wants in the corresponding slots of the Trade menu.**

   The item you want to buy appears on the right side of the menu.

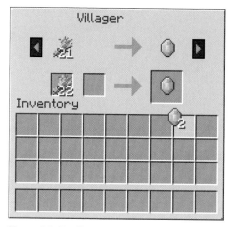

Figure 8-2: Trading

3. **To buy the item that appears, click it.**

If you invest enough resources into the trade for multiple items, Shift-click to buy as much as you can.

4. **Close the Trade menu and wait for a moment. If green sparks appear around the villager (indicating that the villager has unlocked a new trade option), repeat Steps 1 through 3 to trade new items with the villager.**

When you trade with the villager again, use the arrow buttons to cycle through available trades. Some trades close if you use them too many times or if you harm the villager who is offering them.

5. **Find other trading opportunities.**

If you help farm crops in a village, your profits (resulting from farmers buying wheat from you) will fetch you a number of emeralds.

Surviving zombie sieges

Zombies may be no problem for you, but they're quite dangerous to villagers. Zombies chase them and can easily kill cornered villagers. In Normal mode or Hardcore mode, zombies turn these victims into *more* zombies, causing them to form swarms as they tear through the village.

Occasionally, a nearby village experiences a zombie siege at night, in which a horde of zombies appears and gains the ability to break down wooden doors in Normal mode. (They can already do this in Hardcore mode.) During these sieges, the village may lose many inhabitants unless you do something.

Defending a village

Do your best to stop zombie sieges. Use torches to build a somewhat safe zone around the village, and kill off zombie infestations before they can reach villagers and expand. Take extra preemptive measures too, such as building iron golems (described in Chapter 7) and adding extra doors to houses.

Restoring a village

Villagers can repopulate their own cultures, but sometimes a zombie attack will leave an entire population devastated. To restore a village, follow these steps:

1. **Find a zombie villager.**

   This type of villager burns in the daylight, so make sure that a few are indoors. A zombie villager wearing a helmet is also immune to daylight.

2. **Throw a splash potion of weakness at the zombie villager, and then promptly right-click him with a golden apple.**

   The effect from the potion lasts only briefly, so act swiftly with the golden apple. (Chapter 6 has the low-down on potions.)

3. **Wait.**

   The zombie villager shakes slightly and emits red swirls, indicating that he's reverting. Wait it out for a minute or so, and you have a villager.

If the new villagers can remain safe until the zombies have been either converted or slain, you will have restored a village to its former glory.

Building a village

If you can't find a village, build your own. Zombie villagers have the slight possibility of appearing in the same places as zombies do, so if you follow the steps in the preceding section to turn a zombie into a villager, you can start your colony.

A villager needs a home, of course. A villager lives in any enclosed space that has a wooden door. If you add extra doors, more villagers will decide to live in the same building — essentially, a door defines a living space.

After your colony has at least 10 villagers and 21 houses, iron golems may appear and defend your work. You can build a large colony by organizing a large number of houses or by building large manors or apartments that have numerous doors.

Excavating Structures

The village is by far the most advanced structure in Minecraft, but many other types can appear throughout the world. These structures often provide useful materials and can contain treasure chests for you to find.

Desert temple

You occasionally find a sandstone pyramid while exploring the desert. As shown in Figure 8-3, this useful resource is worth excavating.

This pyramid structure is composed of several different types of sandstone, including hieroglyphics that can be collected and used as building blocks. The pyramid, which is a single room with numerous entrances, has a spiral staircase in each of its towers and a secret tunnel leading to four treasure chests.

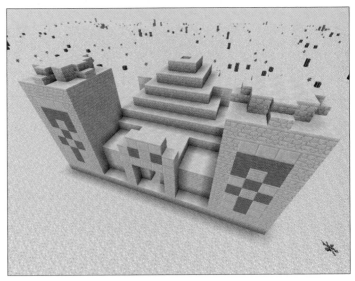

Figure 8-3: Desert temple

You have to dig in the correct spot to find the treasure of the temple. Watch out, though — a long fall and a trap await you. The trap in particular is quite dangerous, using TNT and a pressure plate, but you can scavenge good resources from it.

Though a desert temple can be partially caved in with sand, you can generally see it easily in the flat parts of the desert. Be sure to look for one when you're in the biome.

Jungle temple

The moss-covered jungle temple is much more difficult to find than a desert temple. You can find jungle temples hidden among the trees in the jungle, as shown in Figure 8-4.

The jungle temple is composed primarily of mossy cobblestone, a rare building block. The temple has two floors and a basement: The top floor is a balcony, and the bottom floor holds the empty main room. The basement contains tripwire traps and a couple of secrets. Two treasure chests are available in jungle temples — you can find one in the basement and the other beneath a secret passage on the first floor. To open the secret passage, you have to solve the combination lock in the basement.

Figure 8-4: Jungle temple

If you're not in Adventure mode (described in Chapter 10), you can bypass many jungle temple challenges. Use shears to cut tripwire, and use a pickaxe to smash your way through the combination lock. You can also scavenge useful materials such as dispensers, chiseled stone bricks, and pistons.

Dungeon

The small, rare dungeon structure, shown in Figure 8-5, appears underground as a cobblestone room. It usually has no entrance, so you can use a pickaxe to break in and find treasure chests, which contain moderately useful items. It's also the only way (other than trading) to get the elusive saddle item, which allows you to ride pigs as a means of transport.

The center of the dungeon contains a fiery grate with a spinning figurine in its center. This block sporadically spits out monsters in nearby dark areas. You can break this block quickly with a pickaxe or neutralize it by lighting the area around it. You can also exploit this block's capabilities to obtain loot from the monsters that appear.

Figure 8-5: Dungeon

Mine the mossy cobblestone from the walls because this rare, decorative block can show your explorative prestige.

Witch hut

The rare witch hut structure, which appears propped up on posts in swamps, is used as living space for evil witches, as shown in Figure 8-6. The witch hut — which contains a potted mushroom, a crafting table, and a cauldron — can spawn a witch, as detailed in Chapter 7.

Figure 8-6: Witch hut

This structure is useful because the witch that appears in it drops potion ingredients when it's slain. However, it's also worthwhile to take the cauldron, because it's rather expensive to craft.

Abandoned mine shaft

Large, abandoned mine shafts can be found underground, as shown in Figure 8-7. You can find several useful treasure chests in these complex webs of broken rails and tunnels, and you can forage lots of minecart rails. However, you can also easily get lost.

Figure 8-7: Abandoned mine shaft

While exploring an abandoned mine shaft, you may discover a room packed with cobwebs, which can slow you down considerably. At the center of the cobwebs is a grate, similar to the one inside a dungeon. The grate spawns cave spiders (described in Chapter 7), which are giant, blue bugs that crawl from the cobwebs and attack you. The cave spider's poisonous bite makes it a distinctive threat.

To reach the spawner block and shut it off (by breaking it with a pickaxe or lighting possible spawning areas with torches), hack your way through the cobwebs — a sword does this job quickly. Cobwebs also provide lots of string, which you can use to craft items such as wool, bows, and fishing poles.

Stronghold

The incredibly rare (and giant) Stronghold structure is shown in Figure 8-8. Only three exist in most worlds, and all are generally far away from you at the start of the game. You can find the general direction of one, as detailed in Chapter 3, by right-clicking while holding an eye of ender and watching in which direction it points.

Figure 8-8: Stronghold

The main feature of the Stronghold is that it contains the portal to the End. However, the Stronghold itself has plenty of features to explore, as described in this list:

- **Rooms:** A Stronghold has many rooms, which can contain fountains, prison cells, and stairwells. Most rooms contain lots of high-end building materials, such as iron bars, iron doors, and stone bricks. You can also get mossy stone bricks and cracked stone bricks (building blocks that I could not find elsewhere when I wrote this chapter).

- **Treasure:** Strongholds generate a huge number of valuable treasure chests. Find as many as you can!

- **Libraries:** Sometimes, you find in a Stronghold an abandoned library that contains many bookshelves and, possibly, a balcony and chandelier. The bookshelves are useful to collect, and treasure is hidden throughout the library.

- **Danger:** Use torches to light up the Stronghold quickly! When you break a wall, be careful — a silverfish might pop out and attack you. If you can break a wall quickly with your hand (hold down the left mouse button to see whether the cracks in the block expand quickly), you know that a silverfish is inside.

Nether fortress

The *nether fortress* is a dark, elaborate castle that you can find — where else? — in the Nether. The fortress, which consists of dark rooms and giant bridge-mounted hallways, as shown in Figure 8-9, is important throughout the game because it's home to both Blaze and wither skeletons, as detailed in Chapters 3 and 7, respectively. In certain rooms, you can also find nether wart growing, which you can collect and farm.

Figure 8-9: Nether fortress

9

Playing with MultiPlayer and Cheats

*B*ecause Minecraft rewards creativity and progression toward your own goals, a large part of the accomplishment you may feel during the gameplay stems from being able to share this creativity and progression with friends. In MultiPlayer mode, multiple avatars explore the same world — all online — and collaborate or battle with other people.

Starting or Joining a Multiplayer World

Playing on a Minecraft server has several benefits. For example, you can

✔ Build collaboratively, as shown in Figure 9-1.

✔ Embark on adventures as a team.

✔ Create a town.

✔ Gather and trade resources.

✔ Duel other players.

✔ Chat and hang out.

✔ Use customized gameplay. Some servers use third-party programs that improve their content but don't have to be downloaded.

Figure 9-1: Two players building a house

Minecraft offers several ways to place multiple people in the same world. This section describes them in order of difficulty.

LAN server

On a local area network server — or *LAN* server, as it's commonly known — friends who share the same Internet connection send their avatars into the same world in which you're playing.

Starting your LAN server

To start a LAN server, follow these steps:

1. **Start or continue a world in Minecraft.**

2. **Press Esc to open the Game menu.**

3. **Click the Open to LAN button.**

4. **Select the settings you want and click Start LAN World.**

   Now people who share your network connection can join your server.

Joining another LAN server

Alternatively, if you want to join a LAN server started by someone else, follow these steps:

1. **Select Multiplayer from the main menu.**

    The server list appears. It should be empty if you're just starting in MultiPlayer mode. At the end of the server list, you see the message Scanning for LAN Worlds.

2. **Wait for your friend's LAN world to appear.**

    After a short time, the server list should display a LAN server with your friend's Minecraft username and world name.

3. **Click the server name and then click the Join Server button.**

    Alternatively, simply double-click the server name.

The LAN feature lets you play online any world that normally is single player.

 If the LAN server doesn't appear or you cannot log in, check your Internet connection — you or the server host may have a network problem, or you may be using a different network.

Public server

Of course, you may want a server that can run even when you aren't online, and one that's accessible by people using a different Internet connection. A server of this kind is defined by an IP address or a web address, which is, loosely, a string of characters used to access a port and play online.

Joining a public server

To join a public server, follow these steps:

1. **Select Multiplayer from the main menu.**

    The server list appears. It should be empty if you're starting out in MultiPlayer mode. You can add servers to this list to access them quickly, and you can delete them when you no longer use them or when you want to add them again later.

2. **Click the Add Server button.**

   The Add Server menu appears.

3. **Choose a name and fill out the address.**

   In the Server Name text box, name the server so that you can identify it when it appears in your server list. The Server Address box holds the IP address of the server, which can be shared manually or online. Some servers have websites you can visit to get the address.

4. **Click Done.**

   The server list returns and automatically tests your connection to the server.

5. **After the connection is established, click the server name and then click the Join Server button to start playing.**

The five bars next to a server on the server list monitor your connection to that server. If the bars are crossed out and a red error message appears, your connection may not work, or the server may simply be down temporarily.

A server may not work because it hasn't been updated to the latest version of Minecraft. To continue using a server or an add-on after the game is updated, select the Not Now option when asked whether you want to update Minecraft. This query appears every time you start the game, unless it's already up to date.

Creating your own public server

Creating your own server is more difficult than completing other multiplayer options, and you need to know how to open the 25565 port on your router to run it; this topic is beyond the scope of this book. You can find instructions for downloading the server launcher shown in Figure 9-2 at `www.minecraft.net/download` — port forwarding instructions depend on your router or any third-party program you might use.

To customize a server, see Chapter 10.

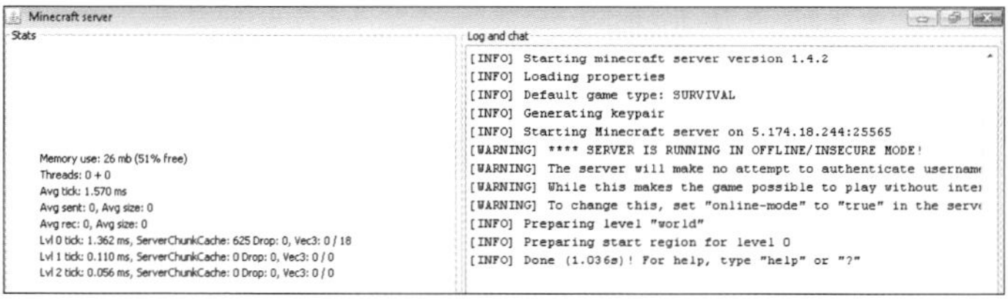

Figure 9-2: Minecraft server interface

Using the Chat Menu

You can communicate with other players or use *cheats* (which cause instant alterations to the world) by pressing T, typing a message, and pressing Enter. Note that if you hide the chat log using the Options menu, you cannot chat.

The Chat menu also allows you to use cheats if the server or world allows it. A cheat is preceded by a slash (/) when entered into the Chat menu — if you're running a public server, the slash is not used.

Use cheats by entering the commands described in the following sections.

Commands that can be used by all players

Any players who are connected to the world can use these commands:

- /help: Display all cheats available to you. If you can't view them all, type **/help 2**, **/help 3**, and so on, to see more. If you're using a public-server launcher, type **help** to view the commands that are accessible from the launcher.

- /kill: Your avatar dies.

- /me: In this third-person form of talking, you type /**me** followed by an action to indicate your avatar emoting. For example, someone named Isometrus would type /me wants cake to make the chat log display * Isometrus wants cake.

- /seed: View the world seed, mentioned in Chapter 10.

✔ /tell: Send a private message that only the target player can read — for example, /tell Isometrus Don't tell anyone, but I hid my diamonds in the basement.

Operator-only commands

An *op* is a person on a public server who has exclusive rights to certain cheats. Ops can be assigned by the server administrator or by other ops. Anyone who is an op and connected to the server can use these commands:

✔ /difficulty: Changes the difficulty of the server — typing /difficulty 0 turns on Peaceful mode, and 1, 2 and 3 refer to Easy, Normal, and Hard, respectively.

✔ /clear: Clears the target player's inventory — for example, /clear Isometrus. You can also add a data value and damage value (see the appendix, available for download at www.dummies.com/go/minecraftfd) to remove only a specific item from a player's inventory. For example, /clear Isometrus 3 removes any dirt blocks from Isometrus's inventory, whereas /clear Isometrus 272 0 removes all unbroken stone swords.

✔ /gamemode: Changes a player's game mode. You can enter Survival mode by typing survival, s , or 0. (Creative is creative, c or 1, and Adventure is adventure, a, or 2.) For example, /gamemode 1 Isometrus sets Isometrus to Creative mode. If you don't enter a player name, the command targets you.

✔ /defaultgamemode: Changes the initial game mode when you log in. For example, /default gamemode s sets all new players to Survival mode.

✔ /gamerule: Changes a game rule. You can further customize the server by entering /gamerule, followed by a rule, followed by either true or false. For example, you can enter /gamerule keepInventory true. The rules that can be changed by using this command are listed in Table 9-1, at the end of this list.

✔ /give: Gives the target player an item. You must know the data value of the item (see the appendix). The full syntax of the /give command is

```
/give <player> <data value> <number of
items> <damage value>
```

You can skip the last two, if you want. For example, /give Isometrus 3 32 places 32 dirt blocks in Isometrus's inventory.

✔ /say: Loudly broadcasts a message, such as /say Server going down in 15 minutes. Typing say <message> into the server launcher sends the message under the username [CONSOLE].

✔ /spawnpoint: Sets a player's spawn point to your current location so that his avatar appears there whenever he dies or joins the world. For example, /spawnpoint Isometrus sets Isometrus's spawn point to your current location. You can also enter coordinates such as /spawnpoint Isometrus 300 60 400 to manually set a spawn point. Coordinates are in the form <x> <y> <z>, where the positive y-axis points toward the sky; press F3 to view your current coordinates.

✔ /time: Changes the time and can be used in many different ways — for example, /time set day and /time set night cause a forced sunrise or sunset. Also, /time set # sets the time manually, where # is a number measured in 20ths of a second and 0 is sunrise. You never have to enter a number larger than 24000, which also forces sunrise. The command /time add # adds the value of # to the current time.

✔ /toggledownfall: Turns rain on or off.

✔ /tp: Followed by two player names, teleports one to the other; for example, /tp Alice Bob teleports Alice to Bob. If you enter only one name, you teleport to the target player. You can also use coordinates such as /tp Isometrus 300 60 400 to teleport a player to a specific point.

✔ /weather: Changes the weather to clear, rainy, or stormy by giving the command /weather clear, /weather rain, or /weather thunder. You can also use a number such as /weather rain 30 to change the weather for a set number of seconds.

✔ /xp: Grants experience orbs to the target player. For example, /xp 500 Isometrus gives Isometrus 500 experience orbs, enough to bring him to Level 23. If no player name is given, the orbs are given to you. You can also type the text /xp 500L Isometrus (or similar) to grant 500 levels rather than 500 orbs.

Table 9-1		Game Rules
Rule	*Default Setting*	*Effect*
command BlockOutput	True	Operators can view the effects of redstone command blocks in the Chat menu. Turn off this setting if you begin receiving spam. These blocks, which activate cheats when given redstone power, can be obtained only by using `/give 137`.
doFireTick	True	Fire spreads, destroys certain blocks, or dies out.
doMobLoot	True	Mobs that are killed can drop items.
doMobSpawning	True	Mobs (described in Chapter 7) appear in the world naturally. When this setting is False, the spawn egg may still be used.
doTileDrops	True	When this setting is False, blocks that are broken cannot produce items.
keepInventory	False	Players who die keep their items.
mobGriefing	True	Blocks are destroyed or moved by creepers, ghasts, endermen, the wither, and the ender dragon.

Operator-only, public-server-only commands

Anyone who is an op can use these commands, though they don't work on LAN servers:

- ✔ `/op`: Followed by a player's username (such as `/op Isometrus`), makes her an operator (or *op*) and allows her to use more cheats. If nobody on the server is an op, type the command (without the slash) into the server launcher shown earlier, in Figure 9-2. To use cheats on a LAN server, click the Allow Cheats button after clicking Open to LAN.

- ✔ `/deop`: Removes a player's operator status; the opposite of `/op`.

✔ /ban: Followed by a player's username (such as /ban Isometrus), bans the player from the server until another op issues a pardon. This technique controls malicious players who damage other players' work or cheat to get ahead. If you want the player to know why he was banned, you can add a reason to your ban, such as /ban Isometrus As an example to the others.

✔ /ban-ip: Bans a specific IP address, preventing a certain computer from connecting to the server. You can't ban offline players with this command.

✔ /banlist: Shows a list of all banned players. Type /banlist ips to list all banned addresses.

✔ /debug: Lets you use /debug start and /debug stop to control debug profiling, if your server behaves erratically.

✔ /kick: Temporarily boots a player from the server. Uses the same syntax as /ban but allows the player to log on again.

✔ /list: Lists all players on the server; however, you can do this easily by pressing the Tab key.

✔ /pardon: Pardons a banned player, allowing him on the server again, using the same syntax as /ban. You can also use /pardon-ip to pardon a banned address.

✔ /save-all: Saves the world in case you have to shut down the server. You can also use /save-off and /save-on to toggle automatic saving. If you're about to make a significant change to the world, you can use /save-off to prevent the world from saving so that you can recover your old world if something goes wrong.

✔ /stop: Saves and shuts down the server.

✔ /whitelist: Produces an optional list of all players who are allowed on the server. (The list of banned players is often known as a *blacklist*.) The command /whitelist on prevents anyone from joining unless she's an op or a member of the whitelist. /whitelist off negates it.

You can type a command such as /whitelist add Isometrus or /whitelist remove Isometrus to change who's allowed on. /whitelist list lets you view the whitelist, and /whitelist reload lets you refresh the whitelist to see whether a banned player can get on the server.

Nonspecific parameters

Many commands ask for the name of a player, such as /tp or /give, but you can instead use a parameter from Table 9-2. For example, the command /tp @a 0 60 0 teleports every player to the center of the map.

Table 9-2	Extra Parameters
Parameter	*Whom It Targets*
@p	The nearest player (in a redstone command block, the player closest to the block)
@r	A random player
@a	All players (repeated for every player online)
@f	The player who's farthest away

10

Customizing Your Experience

In This Chapter

▷ Playing in Hardcore mode or Adventure mode
▷ Starting customized worlds
▷ Managing the `.minecraft` file system
▷ Benefitting from external resources

*1*n addition to Survival mode and Creative mode, Minecraft offers other means for you to experience the game the way you want. You can play in Hardcore mode for an intense survival challenge or play in Adventure mode for a more progressive gameplay style that includes custom maps built by other players. You can also use various means of customizing your multiplayer server. This chapter orients you to all these possibilities.

Surviving Hardcore Mode

When you open the world-creation screen, one difficulty setting for a new world is Hardcore mode, as shown in Figure 10-1.

Figure 10-1: Starting a Hardcore world

Hardcore mode resembles Survival mode (covered in Chapters 1 through 8) but has these differences:

✔ **The game difficulty is set to Hard.** You cannot change the game difficulty. Zombies break down doors, mobs inflict extra damage, and you can die from a lack of food. Creepers are incredibly dangerous in this mode, and they can generally bring you down with one blast.

✔ **Your world is deleted when you die.** Don't dwell on elaborate building procedures, because you have only a single life in Hardcore mode. Stay alive any way you can. If you're on a Hardcore server and you die, you're banned from the server until someone pardons you and lets you try again.

✔ **The hearts on the Health bar look different.** The "angry eyes" on the Health bar indicate that you're in Hardcore mode and that you should preserve your health.

Your experience in Hardcore mode can be rather different from Survival mode. To succeed in Hardcore mode, follow these principles:

✔ **On your first night, find protection and food.** Craft a wooden sword — or a stone one if you have time. Farming is a useful long-term strategy for growing food, but first obtain effective short-term sustenance, such as meat or mushroom stew. Cows are useful because they provide lots of food and makeshift leather armor.

↙ **Find shelter quickly.** The easiest way is to find three sheep as fast as you can and craft a bed. If you use this bed as soon as night falls, you can sleep through the night and not be interrupted by a wandering monster. Alternatively, build a simple house with a light source and fill it with food.

↙ **Start a farm.** Maintaining a consistent food source is essential to thriving in Hardcore mode. (See Chapter 5 for more on farming.)

↙ **Obtain armor.** Find a ravine or a cave with a lot of coal, and craft iron armor as quickly as possible. Wearing armor lowers the chance of being defeated by a few surprise skeletons.

↙ **Avoid creepers.** In Hardcore mode, creepers can kill you with ease, even when you wear armor. Always look around for creepers to prevent them from following you, and use sprinting attacks to knock creepers away from you. If a creeper manages to sneak up on you, move as far as possible from the explosion radius.

Add windows or other features to your house to be able to check for creepers hiding around bends.

↙ **Advance carefully and always have an escape route.** Use lots of torches and scaffolding to navigate caves and obtain high-end minerals, such as redstone or diamond. Use cobblestone to build bridges in the Nether and avoid the danger of falling into lava.

In Hardcore mode, carry flint and steel with you in the Nether — in case you need to reactivate your portal home. One of the worst things that can happen in the Nether (described in Chapter 3) is for a ghast to hit your portal home with a fireball, deactivating it. If all else fails, you can obtain the reagents for a fire charge (see Chapter 4) from wither skeletons, Blaze, and ghasts. Use the fire charge on the portal frame to reactivate it.

Exploring Adventure Mode

Adventure mode — which adds another layer of difficulty to Minecraft — resembles Survival mode except that you cannot break blocks unless you have the proper tool. For example, you can't chop trees without an axe, dig dirt without a shovel, break leaf blocks without shears, or destroy cobwebs without a sword. You can, however, place blocks if you manage to obtain them.

You can start a game in Adventure mode when creating a new world, or you can use the /gamemode cheat (described in Chapter 9) to switch to Adventure mode from any world.

You can advance through the game in Adventure mode, using the help of creepers to break blocks or trading for tools in villages. However, Adventure mode is best used while playing custom maps. (See the section "Checking Out External Sites and Resources," later in this chapter.)

Implementing Additional World Options

In addition to its various game modes, Minecraft has several minor features you can use to further customize your world. When you open the world-creation screen, click the More World Options button (refer to Figure 10-1) to access these features. When creating a world, you can customize it in these five ways, as shown in Figure 10-2:

- ✔ **Seed for the World Generator:** If you see a world you like, you can create a new, identical world. Use the /seed cheat (explained in Chapter 9) to view the world seed and then insert it in this text box at the top of the screen. Use this data (generally, a very large number) as the template for building a world. You can also type a string such as DUMMIES or Test123 into the text box — if it produces an interesting-looking world, share the string with others so that they can reproduce it.

- ✔ **Generate Structures:** Click this button to specify whether structures such as villages (see Chapter 8 for a full list) appear in your world.

- ✔ **World Type:** Click to toggle the world type between Default, Superflat (see the next section), and Large Biomes.

✔ **Allow Cheats:** Click to allow the world cheats specified in Chapter 9. The default setting is On in Creative mode and Off in other modes. You can also enable or disable cheats after converting a world to a LAN server.

✔ **Bonus Chest:** Click this button to make a bonus chest appear next to you when you start creating the world. This storage chest contains useful starting materials.

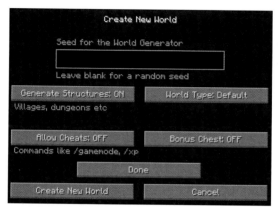

Figure 10-2: Additional world options

Customizing a superflat world

The flattened, single-biome superflat world allows for easier building at the cost of a less natural feel. A superflat world is simply made of stacked layers of blocks. The default flat world is composed of a layer of grass, two layers of dirt, and a layer of bedrock — as well as, occasionally, structures such as trees, dungeons, or villages.

When you select Superflat as the world type when creating a world, you can then click the Customize button to view the current makeup of the world. Click the Presets button to view detailed options for customizing your world, as shown in Figure 10-3.

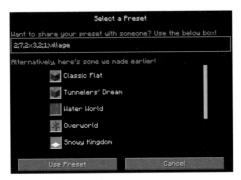

Figure 10-3: Selecting a preset

The text box at the top of the Select a Preset screen shows the code for your world; click the Use Preset button at the bottom of the screen to implement the code. You can also replace it with the code for an interesting world that another player has created and shared. Alternatively, you can select one of the eight default worlds available to you, as described in Table 10-1.

Table 10-1		Preset Worlds
Name	*Biome*	*Description*
Bottomless Pit	Plains	Similar to Classic Flat but with no bedrock layer (so that you might fall through the earth!)
Classic Flat	Plains	A simple, grassy expanse with some villages
Desert	Desert	A desert with villages, pyramids, wells, and underground structures
Overworld	Plains	A flat re-creation of the default Minecraft world, with many of its features
Redstone Ready	Desert	A visually and mechanically perfect world for trying out redstone creations, with villages
Snowy Kingdom	Ice Plains	A cold world that experiences snowfall occasionally

Name	Biome	Description
Tunnelers' Dream	Technically Extreme Hills (different grass color, sparse trees)	A grassy plain with a sparse number of trees, on top of a huge underground with dungeons, mine shafts, and strongholds
Water World	Technically Plains	A deep ocean, home to several interesting villages

To delete a section of a superflat world, select any section on the Superflat Customization screen and click the Remove Layer button.

Making your own options

If Survival mode doesn't provide enough challenge for you, you can always find your own way of taking your experience to the next level. Try to survive without building a house, for example, or live in a cave and never use torches. If you're ever bored, challenge yourself!

Managing the .minecraft Folder

If you want to download maps or texture packs, duplicate or export worlds, reset statistics, or manage screen shots, you use the .minecraft folder. This set of files on your computer contains information about your personalized version of Minecraft and appears in the Users⇨*Username*⇨AppData⇨Roaming folder on your PC. The AppData folder may be hidden, so you can simply search your computer for the phrase *.minecraft.*

Do not edit the files in the .minecraft folder if you don't know what you're doing. If the source files are damaged, you may have to purge Minecraft and download it again. The same advice applies to using the saves folder — at the worst, you may corrupt or lose some of your worlds, rendering them unplayable.

You usually have to close the Minecraft window to be able to make changes to files.

Using .minecraft

You can use the .minecraft file system to further customize your experience, by editing files in a way that's unavailable from within the game. Some of the folders you can edit are described in this list:

- ✔ **bin:** The minecraft file inside this folder contains the heart of your game. At the time of this writing, Minecraft is still releasing new updates, and its creators sometimes release *snapshot* updates that you can download to test upcoming features.

  To use these snapshots, download the new minecraft. jar folder and replace your old one. However, always keep a backup of the original minecraft.jar file, and create new worlds to try out the snapshot so that your old ones don't become corrupted.

- ✔ **saves:** When you open this folder, you find more folders, each one corresponding to one of your worlds. The names of your folders may not correspond with the names of your worlds, especially if either was renamed, but the world-selection screen in Minecraft also displays your folder names in gray under the world names.

  By copying, uploading, or downloading the files (usually in a .zip file) inside these world folders, you can obtain and share custom maps, duplicate worlds, or store backups. To copy a world into saves, simply create a new folder and put the world files in the saves folder, as shown in Figure 10-4.

- ✔ **screenshots:** In this folder, you can find all your screen shots. (Press F2 to take a screen shot.)

- ✔ **stats:** The stats folder contains the data for your progression through the achievements, which loosely guide you through the game, and your statistics, which keep track of how you play. You can view either achievements or statistics by clicking the corresponding button, the Pause menu. If you want to reset your statistics, just delete both files in the stats folder.

- ✔ **texturepacks:** Insert texture packs into your game by placing them here. These groups of folders, images, and other types of files can be imported in a single folder or Zip file. To select a texture pack, click the Texture Packs button on the Options menu and change the general look of the game by giving new images to the surfaces of blocks and entities. Texture packs can be shared by graphical designers — if a pack requires a third-party program to work, follow the extra download instructions that are provided.

Figure 10-4: Managing worlds

Recovering .minecraft

If Minecraft crashes while you're managing the file system, you can try one of these methods to recover your content:

- ✔ **Backtrack to look for conflicts.** Delete any recently downloaded third-party software from the `.minecraft` folder.

- ✔ **Start over.** Back up your worlds, screen shots, and other game elements, and then completely uninstall Minecraft and download it again.

- ✔ **Search for your specific error online.** For example, if Minecraft displays an error message when you continue a world, you can search for the error message online and see what other players have to say.

Checking Out External Sites and Resources

Some truly amazing websites — such as Minecraft Forums (`www.minecraftforum.net/forum`) and Minecraft Wiki (`www.minecraftwiki.net`) — focus on Minecraft, providing information, discussion, and downloads of third-party programs. As long as you have an Internet connection and a search engine, you can use various Minecraft websites to complete these tasks:

- ✔ **Ask for help:** A lot of people have helpful opinions on the more advanced concepts of Minecraft.

- ✔ **Discuss ideas:** Share your Minecraft fandom with others.

- ✔ **Play custom maps:** Lots of people build maps that add extra challenge to the game or create a whole new way of playing it. (The earlier section "Managing the .minecraft Folder" explains how to download them.) Maps that require extra third-party programs to play should provide specific instructions.

- ✔ **Download mods and texture packs:** Though texture packs are covered in this chapter, *mods* are extra bits of code that add content to the game. See the individual mods for download information.

- ✔ **Customize your skin:** Change your avatar's look by downloading a skin or making your own in an image editing program. You can find instructions at www.minecraft.net/profile.

- ✔ **Build and share:** Connect to the community via forums, servers, or other types of social media to optimize your Minecraft experience.

In addition, the Minecraft community has found many ways to connect Minecraft with real life, by building famous architectural structures in Creative mode and using Minecraft as an educational tool, a supplemental resource, and more. As long as you have an Internet connection, you have an outlet to a vast and creative community.

11

Ten Helpful Survival Tips

*M*any components of Minecraft connect with each other, so a variety of helpful procedures have been discovered. Though clever players have discovered many helpful tips, the ten in this chapter should provide a better survival experience.

Digging Safely

The underground in Minecraft presents quite a bit of danger, so mine carefully to avoid these common hazards:

✓ **Falling when digging straight down:** Breaking the block underneath you always increases the danger of falling into a pit or a pool of lava. Staircase mines (described in Chapter 5) are useful because they don't require you to dig straight down.

✓ **Falling sand and gravel or flowing lava when digging upward:** Be sure to quickly stopper flowing lava with blocks such as cobblestone.

If you follow basic safety guidelines, you can navigate dark caves and huge lava lakes with no problem.

Cooking Efficiently

Sometimes, you want to cook or smelt a large amount of material, such as beef to turn into steak or sand to burn into glass.

Because you need a furnace and a good source of fuel for this task, managing fuel efficiently is obviously an important skill.

You can cook with coal or any other hot or flammable material. The best resources to use are the wooden plank (cooks 3 items for every 2 planks), coal (cooks 8 items per lump), the blaze rod (cooks 12 items per rod), and the lava bucket (cooks 100 items). The latter two resources are useful only if you've spent time in the Nether — a dimension that can also provide a good source of coal, from wither skeletons, as described in Chapter 7.

In addition, you can cook one item using two saplings, so you can use saplings to your advantage if you don't need them for anything else. You can also cook an item with a wooden tool, providing a use for a neglected or near-broken wooden pickaxe.

 You can also smelt logs into charcoal, which is slightly more efficient — but more time-consuming — than converting them into planks. This trick is probably more useful for crafting torches and similar items.

Obtaining Obsidian and Portals Quickly

If you're playing in Survival mode and you're itching to go to the Nether (you can find more information about it in Chapter 3), gather obsidian as fast as possible. Even if you can't find the diamond you need for a pickaxe, you can still build a portal as long as you can find some lava.

Simply use a bucket to place some still lava in the location where you want to place the obsidian, and then dump water over the lava to harden it. Use cobblestone or another non-flammable block to form the "mold" for the portal and the container for the lava, as shown in Figure 11-1.

Figure 11-1: Building a portal mold

Mining in the Right Location

Denser ores such as redstone and diamond appear deep underground, but they're statistically common about 10 blocks above the bedrock layer. However, this spot is also abundant in lava, which you can (mostly) evade by remaining 13 blocks above bedrock. To find a good spot to mine, you can dig down to this level — either descend to bedrock and then move back up 13 blocks, or press F3 and dig until your y-coordinate is 13 — or find a sufficiently deep cave. Digging a tunnel stays more consistently at this depth, though a cave provides a larger surface area to search for minerals.

Avoiding Overexertion

An action such as sprinting or jumping or suffering damage makes you hungry very quickly. Hunger can become irritating when you need a lot of food in order to stay on your feet. Follow these guidelines to avoid exerting yourself:

✔ **Build roads with slabs and stairs.** These elements can help you move around without jumping.

✔ **Connect your destinations with a minecart track.** This strategy is helpful if you have to travel a long distance several times.

✔ **If you're using a staircase mine, use actual stair blocks.** Then you can leave your mine without having to jump.

Defeating Basic Mobs

You have to face zombies, skeletons, spiders, and creepers many times during your Minecraft experience. (See Chapter 7 for more on mobs.) Each creature requires you to have a unique fighting style in order to defeat it. This list describes how to defeat each of these enemies (in order from least to most threatening):

✔ **Zombie:** Sprint and attack this enemy to knock it backward, and jump and attack repeatedly to drain its health. Knock back the closest ones to keep the shape of the group manageable.

✔ **Spider:** Sprint-attack it! Try to predict its jumps, and never let it gain the higher ground. Try to kill the spider quickly with a powerful sword because it has a low health level.

✔ **Creeper:** Sprint and attack the creeper to prevent it from exploding near you. (It's extremely harmful.) If you don't care how you kill it, try to lure it into exploding. If your timing is accurate, you can use creepers to destroy other pursuing mobs, especially spiders.

✔ **Skeleton:** This archer works best alone. Try to situate yourself so that another mob is positioned between you and the skeleton — it sometimes shoots its own teammates! Use items such as blocks and trees to your advantage, by hiding behind them so that the skeleton has to move close to you. If you're near a skeleton, simply kill it as fast as you can. Don't sprint-attack, or else the skeleton gains more shooting space.

In addition, you can defeat a lot of these mobs easily by beating them into pits, cacti, or lava.

Amassing Colored Wool

To build colorful rugs or tapestries, or other visually appealing collections of blocks, you need wool and dye, neither of which is quickly obtained. However, one strategy lets you quickly get any color you want, by using only a few dyes.

When you right-click sheep while holding dye, their wool color changes at a biological level. Therefore, when sheep are shorn, their wool grows back in the same color, and lambs share the same wool color as a parent. Use wheat to lure sheep into multiple fenced-in areas with grass flooring, dye them various colors, and let them breed. To get colored wool, shear the sheep of that color. Shorn sheep regrow their (renewable) wool after eating grass.

Having too many sheep may cause lag and prevent animals from naturally appearing nearby. Spread out your sheep pens and keep only a few of each color.

Crafting Quickly

You can craft material in several ways:

- ✔ **Right-click a bunch of materials to split them in half.** Even if the materials are in the crafting grid, you can craft many items at a time, such as slabs or ladders.

- ✔ **Shift-click surplus materials when you finish crafting.** This action returns them to your inventory.

- ✔ **Craft several items at a time.** Figure 11-2 shows an efficient way of crafting three tools at a time. When you take the axe, the remaining materials form a hoe, and the layer beneath it forms a shovel.

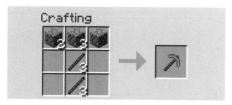

Figure 11-2: Crafting an axe, a hoe, and a shovel

Checking Basic Equipment

After playing Minecraft for a while and growing more confident in your ability to survive, you can keep more items in your inventory and worry less about losing them. Then you can work more efficiently and return home less often.

Always carry certain equipment and supplies on a Minecraft exploration — as long as you know how to keep them safe:

- **Food:** Carry food that you have an abundance of and that doesn't waste inventory space, such as bread or meat.

- **Weaponry:** Keep a sword ready, and possibly a bow or armor. Place a sword in the first slot of your inventory so that you can access it by pressing the 1 key.

- **Pickaxe, axe, and shovel:** Gathering materials while you're exploring is always useful, and if you ever need to break a block, you should have the proper tool ready, for efficiency's sake. A pickaxe is vital in underground areas.

- **Torches:** Never go mining without several torches to light the area.

- **Compass:** You can memorize the coordinates of your house (press F3 to view them) so that you can always return home. If this suggestion doesn't appeal to you, take along a compass instead in case you get lost.

For recipes for these items, check out the appendix, available for download at www.dummies.com/go/minecraftfd.

Finding Natural Comfort

If you need shelter before dark in the hills or the jungle for safety overnight, find an enclosed area (a shallow cave, natural copse, or large tree) and fill in the cracks with blocks to form a natural-looking house.

Index